Architecture as Art

ARCHITECTURE AS ART

THE WORK OF STEPHEN M. SULLIVAN

ORO

ORO Editions — Novato, California

ORO Editions
Publishers of Architecture, Art, and Design
Gordon Goff, Publisher

www.oroeditions.com
info@oroeditions.com

Published by ORO Editions

Project Editor: Clare Jacobson
Managing Editor: Jake Anderson
Book Design: Pablo Mandel

Typeset in Adobe Garamond and Trajan

10 9 8 7 6 5 4 3 2 1 FIRST EDITION

ISBN 978-1-951541-58-3

Color Separations and Printing: ORO Group Ltd.
Printed on TK
Bound in TK
Printed in China.

ORO Editions makes a continuous effort to minimize the overall carbon footprint of its publications. As part of this goal, ORO Editions, in association with Global ReLeaf, arranges to plant trees to replace those used in the manufacturing of the paper produced for its books. Global ReLeaf is an international campaign run by American Forests, one of the world's oldest nonprofit conservation organizations. Global ReLeaf is American Forests' education and action program that helps individuals, organizations, agencies, and corporations improve the local and global environment by planting and caring for trees.

To my daughters,
Perrin Teal-Sullivan and Quill Teal-Sullivan,
and my granddaughter,
Rowan Teal-Sullivan

The Tea Bowl

Drinking tea all day
from this small cup,
searching,
like I had never drawn before.

Holding each idea: new.
This cup takes me to the land
of my masters,
where even not knowing
is done with care.

CONTENTS

Preface *8*

INTUITION *11*

- Engawa Residence *15*

SITE ENERGY *35*

- Anamcara Residence *39*
- Miller Bay Residence *57*

ORDER *67*

- Blue Atlas Residence *71*
- Asgard Residence *85*

NARRATIVE *99*

- Mercer Island Residence *103*

INTEGRATION *119*

- Cliff Residence *123*
- Historic Structures *137*
- Small Houses *157*

Acknowledgments *171*

Catalog of Selected Works *173*

Notes *188*

Credits *190*

PREFACE

The Fairbanks House, Dedham, Massachusetts, 1641.

My personal history informs my view of architecture as art. As a child I lived in a home filled with the handwork of my artist mother, who had a passion for the traditional decorative arts of New England. My engineer father taught me and my siblings how to draw. The aesthetic act was woven into the course of every day. To make things with my hands was as ordinary as sitting down to a meal at the family table.

I grew up in Andover, Massachusetts, before suburbanization altered the balance between the town's long history and modern times. As a boy, I could saunter for miles through woods and fields, observing along the way examples of America's earliest houses, barns, and stone walls and its ancient trees. Some of my family's neighbors had lived in their houses and farmed their fields for generations. Some of the witch trials of the 1600s had been held in this town. The old houses were witnesses to centuries of history and inhabitation.

Curiously to me, even Andover's mid-twentieth-century houses hewed to the pattern of the old ones. The new mimicked the old because of an unspoken societal agreement to work within the tried and true patterns of the past, with a conformity that seems to be almost foreign to our contemporary culture. The local house types were consistent and familiar.

The town plan of North Andover, with a central common green space lined with trees, was still visible. On the edge of town, more than a thousand acres of natural woodland had been put aside in the nineteenth century, inspired by Henry David Thoreau's recommendation that "Each town should have a park, or rather a primitive forest, of five hundred or a thousand acres...where a stick should never be cut for fuel...a common possession forever, for instruction and recreation."[1] These strong patterns of town design and architecture, preserved over generations and centuries, are indelible in my memory of the place. They influenced my interest in architecture and landscape design as a young person.

I attended high school at Phillips Academy Andover, on a campus whose core had been renovated by the great neoclassical architect Charles A. Platt. In the early twentieth century, Platt had moved several of the eighteenth-century brick buildings that had formed the original campus and had added new ones to form a larger plan of quadrangles and vistas. He created an unparalleled vision of the ideal neo-Georgian academic campus, not unlike what Thomas Jefferson had provided at the University of Virginia. All this was intended as a setting for the education of teenage boys. The theory was that the end result of education depended upon the quality of what you gave students early on.

I remember vividly the watercolor renderings for the buildings Platt designed on campus in the early 1900s. They were hung on the staircase walls of the main hall. Climbing to my balcony perch for daily school assembly, these beautiful paintings had a subliminal effect on my awareness of the architecture around me. They instructed me that the beauty of my surroundings was brought forth by the creative minds of artists and builders, for the sake of edifying the minds and lifting the spirits of kids like me.

These two influences, the vernacular pattern of New England domestic architecture and the canonical expression of classicism in the neo-Georgian architecture of the academy, provided me with powerful visual lessons.

While the academic campus expressed a heightened language of history, hierarchy, scale, and proportion, the most ancient of the town's houses displayed an organic connection to their sites. I was shaped by this architectural heritage of a New England town. As Winston Churchill said, as he faced rebuilding the UK Commons Chamber after its destruction during the Blitz in 1943, "We shape our buildings and afterwards our buildings shape us."[2]

In 1973, just out of college, I set off for a year in Japan under the auspices of the Thomas J. Watson Fellowship. The subject of my study was Japanese folk pottery. I intended to travel to as many of the ancient kiln sites as I could during the following year, and to find a place where I might serve an apprenticeship. It was a transformative year of immersion in another culture, its language, and its arts. Japan, and especially its ceramic arts, had long held a fascination for me. By choosing to study folk pottery, I was also choosing to look at the ancient traditions of Japan, still alive and vital despite industrialization and the impact of the Pacific War.

The folk pottery villages were scattered throughout Japan, its kilns dating back many centuries. They tended to be located in remote places, where clay was abundant and where potters could both farm and make their wares. Thus my year of study also necessarily involved visiting and living in traditional agricultural towns, surrounded by rice fields and hills of clay.

For much of that year, I lived in thatched-roof farm buildings whose sheltering forms were like the hills themselves. The simplicity and beauty of the timber frames holding up the steep pitches, the delicacy of sliding wall screens separating room from room, inside from outside, and the ubiquitous veranda, or *engawa,* with polished wood floor holding the edge between the house and the garden made lasting impressions on me. Each day was an education in language, in a different cultural perspective, and in aesthetic sensibility, not to mention the techniques learned daily at the potter's wheel.

I was immersed in an aesthetic tradition that affected everything I saw: architecture, garden design, and the arts (where no distinction was made between "fine" art and craft). I immersed myself in the world of Kyoto and its ancient temples and gardens. The aesthetic of the Zen temple and its garden, where I studied meditation, supported eloquently its spiritual teachings about letting go. Thanks to the kindness and friendship of my sensei, Tatsuzo Shimaoka, and his family, I was deeply welcomed in Japan.

I came to see architecture not as separate from its garden or its larger landscape, but as a variant of an aesthetic attitude to all materiality. My year in Japan moved me forward in my historical and technical understanding of the ceramic arts. But more than this, the experience led me to a way of seeing. This way, new to me, was not so much a nostalgia for the old ways, but rather an observation of what it might take, aside from historic mimicry, to create an aesthetic that was truly embedded in its locality.

After returning from my apprenticeship in Japan, and upon graduating from architecture school, I ultimately settled in the Puget Sound region of Washington State. I came to Lopez Island in the San Juan Islands, at the Canadian border, which has remained my spiritual home since. Settled in the nineteenth century by fruit farmers on the traditional lands of Coast Salish people, the islands even now have a pastoral ambiance due to their remoteness from the mainland. Inland farm valleys, with long vistas to neighboring islands and across the Strait of Juan de Fuca to the snow-capped massif of the Olympic Peninsula, contrast with the coastal bedrock carved by retreating glaciers millennia ago. Due to the difficulty of using materials from elsewhere, the native vernacular buildings tend to be made of glacial fieldstone and wood (cedar and fir). Some of the small houses illustrated here reflect this elemental approach to material choices, scale, and form. The landscape qualities inherent to these islands—the lush evergreen forests, the mossy outcroppings of bedrock, and the ever-present edge of the sea—have made a lasting impression on my work as an architect. They educate my endeavor to build an architecture of place.

The Shimaoka compound in Mashiko, Japan, 1973.

INTUITION

AT THE INITIATION OF an architectural design project, the client and I come together as if at a trailhead to the wilderness. We carry with us our loads of what seem necessary for the adventure of discovery.

In my experience, the client most often comes forward with a specific site that they own for the purpose of building. They also sometimes have a rough sense of what they would like to build upon it as their home. This may include a list of rooms—a program of spaces and sizes that they deem necessary to hold their activities and their repose. They may also carry a list of possessions—works of art, books, or machines—that hold a claim on the spaces they wish to build.

Sometimes they bring with them a preconception of the building's stylistic expression. Clients have approached me with visual memories of places or a time in history that they feel expresses either their self-perception or something of importance to them. I have been asked to work with references to architecture of the Georgian period and to New England, Tuscany, and Japan. Beyond these stylistic roadmaps lie visual associations of importance to the client. These may touch on such themes as durability and history (Georgian or classical, for example), or they may be connected with a refined aesthetic sensibility and material palette (such as Japanese).

These associations are ambassadors of the memories we all hold from our past, which promise comfort or a feeling of peace, or who we imagine ourselves to be or how we wish to be perceived. They are, in a way, intuited and brought forward in my initial dialog with a client as a means of communicating important values. These intuited messages are part of the nonrational process of association that allows the dialog to begin the journey, much like a topographic map of a wilderness trail.

I have always found this moment of the initiation of the project to be the most exciting and the most laden with possibilities. Submitting the process of design to the unknowable outcome is a necessary step. Naturally, I carry many preconceptions—my clients' ("I want my home to look like…") as well as my own—into the process. I try to put these aside as I begin the analytical phase of site design, because experience has shown me that unless the building is intimately tuned to the site and the sun, it will not be successful. I do not want other considerations to interfere with this phase of design inquiry.

I try to allow my and my clients' preconceived notions to have their moment on the stage of consideration without holding onto them. It is not unlike the practice of meditation, in which one permits distracting thoughts to simply float through one's awareness and recognizes them for what they are: merely thoughts that require no action. Letting go of preconceptions allows for an expanded field of perception and enhances the insights of intuitive thinking.

I learned the importance of intuition as a student. My teacher in Japan, Tatsuzo Shimaoka, wrote about the consequence of *tariki* (the other power) in his work as a ceramic artist. In the traditional world of Japanese ceramics, there is a literal submission of the handmade work to the intense heat of the wood fire. The fire has a power that, while controllable to some extent, brings with it an unexpected result—a result sometimes better than previously imagined and perhaps not reproducible, even in identical circumstances.

Shimaoka tutored me by his example of letting go into this other power, and I learned that by submitting patiently to its uncertainty—its unpredictability—something authentic that is beyond the predetermined outcome of a more rational approach may be born.

Another important lesson on intuition came from Bartlett H. Hayes Jr., my teacher at Phillips Academy Andover. He felt that art education was necessary for developing a mind that could make intuitive leaps of discovery, as discoveries in all fields of inquiry—the sciences, medicine, technology—require that the creative mind leap beyond what is obvious through rational observation.

There is a place for rational analysis, of course, in architectural design. Yet it is the play between the rational, predictable inquiry and the surprises of insight of the intuitive process that leads the creative collaboration toward the unique outcome that a particular place, a moment in time, and a unique client may bring forth. Houses are not, after all, merely engineering problems to be solved with a rational plan and a form that elevates the plan into a three-dimensional structure. They are containers of the soul, and they express something of their inhabitants. They are also vessels that convey the energy of the site inward to the inhabitants, allowing them to experience the natural gifts of a place.

Getsu: *wheel-thrown, wood-fired, porcelain vessel.*

ENGAWA RESIDENCE

Seattle, Washington — 2009

OVER THE COURSE OF FOUR YEARS, the clients of the Engawa Residence and I enjoyed an in-depth conversation about the expressive possibilities of architecture and engaged in rich collaborations with other designers, craftspeople, artists, and builders. At the outset of our conversations, the clients asked that the design acknowledge in some way principles of Japanese architecture. For me, the essence of Japanese domestic architecture is epitomized by the space called the *engawa*: the sun-filled edge of a dwelling that connects house to garden, inside to outside, form to spirit. This idea is most directly expressed in the glassy openness of the lake side of this home.

I developed the scheme by means of a typical analysis of the site's characteristics—sunlight, views of the lake and the mountains, important trees to be protected, neighborhood context—and the program of required interior and exterior spaces. There was, more importantly, a parallel process to this analytic one—an intuitive process by which the analytical solutions took on visible form. This phase of the design was unpredictable, open to possibility, and always subject to change. The visual form of this house represents the sometimes harmonious and sometimes clashing needs of these parallel paths of design.

The site's configuration allowed for a plan of two wings intersecting in an obtuse angle, which formed a southeast facing lakeside garden. The plan engages its site with a circulation path along this outside edge, which mimics the experience of the *engawa*. The central organizing space in both the plan and the section of the building is a light core, which I designed as a vessel bringing light into the center of the house at all times of the day. It is a three-dimensional timber-framed structure holding up the central and highest tier

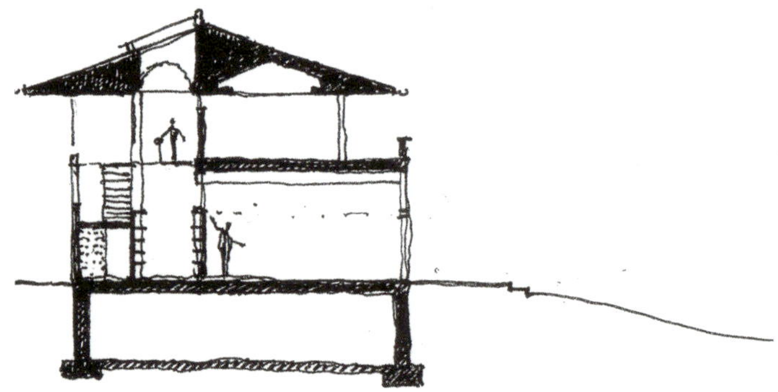

Preliminary section showing the light core.

of the roof. It is the vertical axis of the composition. It serves as the formal path of circulation both horizontally and vertically. It contains the clients' cherished book collection and the family piano. It is the heart of the house. The design also introduces western light by means of a two-story entry, a lantern-like space that is intended to catch the low-angled light of afternoon.

Other references to Japanese architecture can be seen in the house's layered horizontal roof forms, the timber framing of the light core (reminiscent of timber-framed Japanese farmhouses), the horizontal fenestration, the use of screening devices, and the celebration of wood as a primary material. Wood is also a reflection of the clients' family tradition in the wood business. The clients' knowledgeable participation in the selection of wood species, detailing of glued-laminated timber frame, and choices of graining patterns were key elements in establishing the feeling of the interior spaces. This may be observed in the main room with its ceiling of layered hemlock beams and planking.

Board-formed concrete is used for the masses of the chimneys, the site walls, and the four heroic pylons supporting the exterior edge of the main living room. Concrete was used because of both its plasticity as a material and its expression of the wood grain of its formwork. At the front entry door, cast-bronze hardware manifests the impression of a rope, rolled into a clay mold for the casting process. I believe in the importance of craftsmanship in elevating the common materials of wood, concrete, and glass so that they may speak out poetically about the art of construction. The detailing of the design of the Engawa Residence is spare in order for the materials to be experienced in their essential simplicity.

Schematic sketch of roof forms.

ABOVE *Board-formed concrete pylons support the overhanging roof.*
OPPOSITE *The* engawa, *the sun-filled edge of a Japanese dwelling that connects house to garden, inside to outside, form to spirit.*

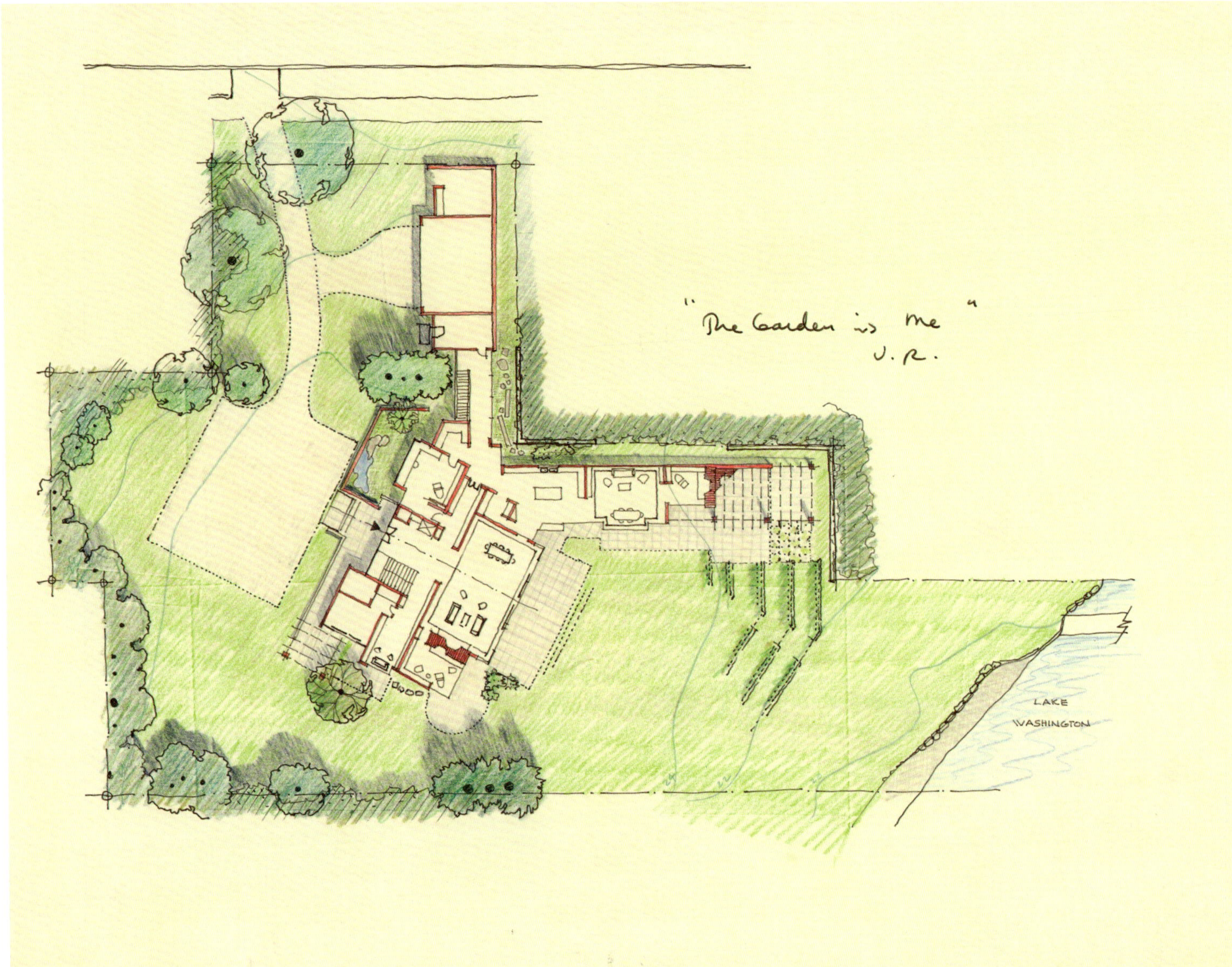

ABOVE *Preliminary site plan with solar diagram.*
OPPOSITE *The great room's layered ceiling is made of hemlock beams and planking.*

ANDO

ANDO

OPPOSITE *The cast-in-place concrete chimney expresses the grain and layers of its wood form boards.* RIGHT *The timber-framed light core supports the top tier of the roof and holds a washi paper sculpture by Kyoko Ibe.*

Rope impressions on clay are of the earliest artistic marks made by humans.

LEFT *A steel staircase runs between a cast-glass railing and a wood screen.*
RIGHT *The light core ascends three stories, to the rooftop.*

SITE ENERGY

My process of architectural design begins with a careful analysis of the site and its particular characteristics. I must discover the unique spirit of a place before I can engage in designing a successful solution for setting a building on the land.

The art of site design is as ancient as the human need to create shelter. It includes such traditions as geomancy, feng shui, and vastu shastra. These traditions relate to the energy of a site and its constituent parts, as well as to its relationship with the larger landscape. Even individual rocks and trees and topographic features will apply an energetic pulse on a place. As Russell Page, the great twentieth-century British garden designer, stated, "There is one aspect of Japanese gardens from which I have learned much, and that is the relationship between objects in space.... [E]very object emanates—sends out vibrations beyond its physical body which are specific to itself. These vibrations vary with the nature of the object."[3]

If a building is to become part of a harmonious whole with its site, then its designer must start by understanding the site's energetic fields. These fields include the solar energy falling on the locale, prevailing patterns of wind, topography, significant vegetation, and the opening of the site to views. Each of these fields can be imagined as exerting forces upon the site as well as upon each other. The concept of genius loci—the protective spirit of a place—summarizes the aggregation of these forces into a coherent whole. The land has a voice that seeks engagement and respect.

When I embark on the analysis of a particular site, I develop a series of preliminary sketches that focus my attention on the characteristics that comprise the essential qualities of the place. In the act of drawing the diagrams, I revisit the site in my mind and begin to process each investigation as a parallel inquiry with all the others, building an understanding of the place layer upon layer. There is no better way to learn the secrets of a spot than to spend time there, especially to sleep there. I have camped on a client's site as a first step in getting to know its qualities intimately. In a rural site on Washington's San Juan Islands, I observed deer bedding down at night, leaving their imprint in the tall grasses. Their path was like a map of their secret knowledge of how and where to feel safe when darkness descended. It is this kind of knowledge that I seek when I determine the right place to build.

I begin my analysis by recognizing that sunlight—the source of life itself—is our most important consideration. Home builders want to orient their living and sleeping spaces with regard to the course of the sun through the sky. Orientation to the sun, and to the gift of its light, is the fundamental ordering decision the designer makes. This idea has a long history: Andrea Palladio, the great Renaissance architect, devoted his attention to the solar orientation of rooms in the Second Book of his famous *The Four Books on Architecture.*

By means of careful attentiveness to the sun's course through the sky, to the natural attributes of a site, and to a choreography of movement through space, I want to craft buildings as vessels of experience that lead the inhabitant to see anew. The design process thus begins by observing the light that falls from the sun onto the site. In my practice I use computer-generated studies to precisely model the solar impact on the building throughout the year. I attempt to balance the need to let in as much winter sun as possible with

Tsuchi: *coil-built, wood-fired vessel, showing marks of the flames.*

the need for summer shade. Creating outdoor spaces with varying levels of sun exposure and shade is enhanced by the solar studies. Using the precision of this type of design tool, I can adjust the fenestration and roof overhangs to optimize solar orientation. I use the same tool to study the shading impact of both the existing vegetation as well as landscape design concepts for the locations of trees.

In our time of diminishing natural resources, designing in such a way that our buildings receive energy from the sun, both passively and actively, as well as use the earth's thermal resources offers a way forward. In my current projects I strive for efficient thermal envelopes, triple glazing of windows, ground source energy use, and both active and passive solar systems.

In the Pacific Northwest where I work, we have a nine-month heating season. I therefore design windowed surfaces to maximize receiving the energy of the sun. To block the sun's harshness during the months of July through September, I use sun-shading overhangs. When my work moves from the cloudy Pacific Northwest to, for example, the Sonoran Desert of Arizona, my approach to the design reflects the changes to the local presence of the sun. In most of my designs, light determines the basic form of the building.

Houses embody the interface between the outer environment and the inner protected environment, and, at the same time, they mediate between the public and the private realms. My analysis of spatial sequence, as it relates to the site, begins to address the threshold between these realms. The concept of liminality (which comes from the Latin *limin* meaning threshold) is used in anthropology and psychology to describe a state of ambiguity, where one moves from one state of being to another. This is a useful concept in considering the experience of arrival, both to a site as well as to a building. As we cross the threshold, we leave the known and enter the unknown. We reveal spatial sequences by moving through liminal markers, whether they are gateways, doorways, anterooms, hallways, or courtyards.

The spatial sequence of the site at the larger scale of landscape (moving from the public realm to the private realm) parallels the development of spatial sequence of the house itself (moving from the entry to the public spaces of the home, and thence to increasingly intimate family spaces). While the experiences of designing for rural, suburban, or urban sites are significantly different, all sites need a careful spatial sequence of arrival and entry in both their landscape design and architectural design to prepare us to arrive.

The interface between the site choreography and the spatial choreography of a house begins to form an architecture tuned uniquely to its place. This is why different projects from my office take on languages of their own, and why each project expresses its unique response to its environmental variables.

ANAMCARA RESIDENCE

Scottsdale, Arizona — 2017

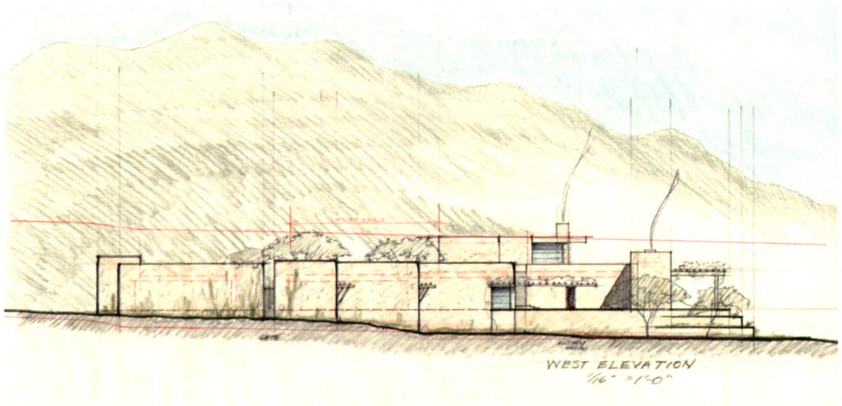

LEFT *Preliminary sketch of the west elevation.*
RIGHT *The harsh afternoon sun on the west elevation necessitated a protective facade with minimal fenestration.*

THE ANAMCARA RESIDENCE is located in Arizona's Sonoran Desert, an iconic landscape of the American West. Tucked up against the McDowell Mountains, it sits on a high plateau overlooking Scottsdale and Phoenix to the south. The site is graced with a feeling of refuge, sheltered by the hills and with a prospect of a hundred miles to the south. The presence of the totemic form of Pinnacle Peak and surrounding mountains within its immediate northerly view and its adjacency to the land preserve of the Reata Wash add to the distinction of place. It is an oasis in the desert, green with an abundance of plant life. There is an element of wildness in the place.

Two primary influences of nature—the unforgiving sun of the desert and the periodic flash flooding of the adjacent Reata Wash—carved the form of the Anamcara Residence.

First, the house is tuned to provide direct sunshine inside in the winter months and to completely shade the living spaces from direct sunlight in the hot months. The building's south elevation faces a desert preserve. Deep overhangs on this south side create outdoor living spaces and a zone of shade. An opening in the protective mass of the building allows light into a central tree-shaded courtyard with a water feature. The courtyard is the symbolic center of the home and marks the point of arrival to a place of sanctuary. It is also the central reference point of the plan, creating a sense of orientation at all times. The courtyard scheme recalls one of the earliest forms of domestic architecture in many cultures.

Solar studies were made to determine precisely when the building's windows were exposed to the sun so that shading strategies could be devised to mitigate heat gain. The exact dimension of each overhang correlates to

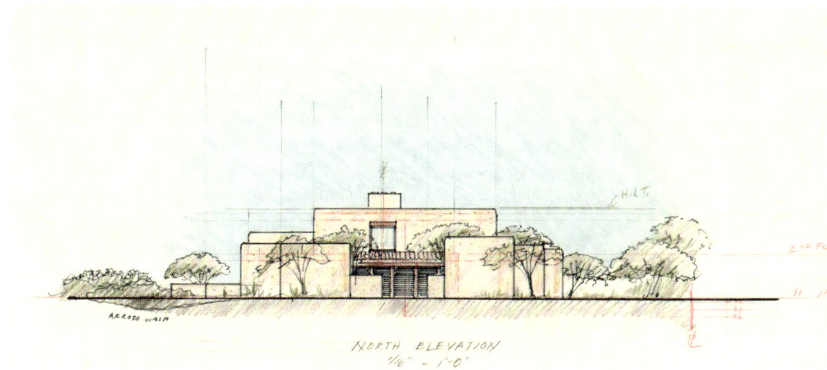

LEFT *The courtyard centers the form of the house, which comprises simple cubic volumes, recalling ancient desert dwellings.*
RIGHT *Schematic massing sketch of entry elevation.*

provide one hundred percent sun protection of the glass during the hot season. The precise tuning of the building to the sun by means of shading devices combined with its massive and heavily insulated walls are timeless strategies for the conservation of energy. An array of photovoltaic cells on the roof provides for active generation of solar power.

Second, the potential for seasonal flooding required that the dwelling be built in such a way that the floor level would be above a hundred-year flood. This necessitated designing a base plinth upon which the structure of the house would sit. This plinth mediates between the level of the home and that of the desert floor by means of a series of planted terraces. The plantings of the terraces integrate this defensive hydrological engineering feat into the visual texture of the desert.

The orientation of the primary spaces is to the southeast. This is the most benevolent direction of the sun in this desert environment and has the benefit in feng shui of orienting these spaces toward the new coming day. The three main spaces along this southeast edge (the Zen room, living room, and kitchen) form a spatial zigzag allowing each space to have both an east and a south wall exposed to the view. This diagonal arrangement of space is derived from both the site orientation as well as the desire for engagement with nature. Thus, the landscape, the flood plinth, and the building are integrated, by means of their intentional references and adjustments to their specific environment, to form an architectural whole.

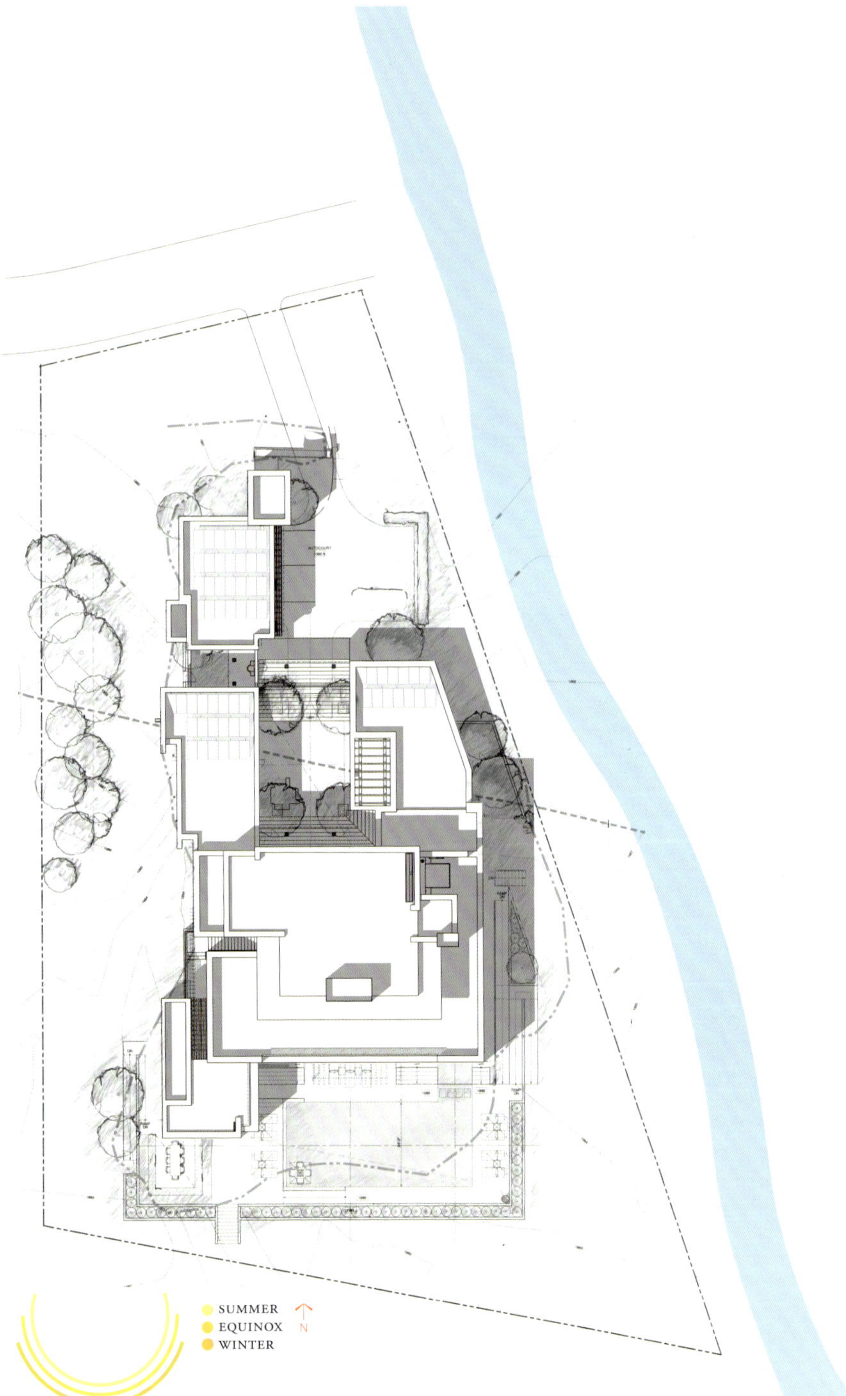

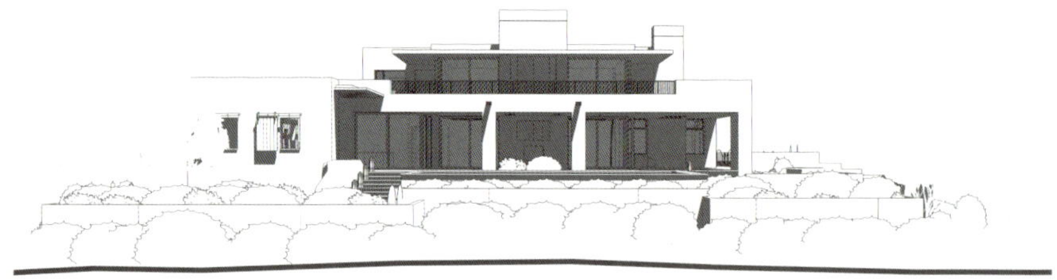

SUMMER

WINTER

OPPOSITE *Site plan with solar diagram and sun studies.*
BELOW *Large outdoor rooms, shaded by deep overhangs, engage the house's south-facing terraces.*

BELOW *This 1925 photograph by Edward S. Curtis of North Pueblo at Taos, reflecting the aggregation of cellular cubic forms, was an inspiration for the massing of the entry elevation.*
RIGHT *Simple cubic forms, a spare material palette, and native Sonoran desert plants create a harmonic relationship between building and setting.*

LEFT *A timber-framed entry porch creates a transition to a private entry courtyard.*
BELOW *Small windows have steel screens based on traditional Moroccan tile patterns.*

BELOW *A stone ramada provides protection from the hot sun on the southwest corner.*
RIGHT *The pool terrace is a desert oasis.*

RIGHT *An exterior passage is protected from afternoon sun by a massive wall of local stone.*
OPPOSITE *The stair hall is illuminated by a slot skylight that minimizes heat gain while providing a solar feature at the landing wall.*

MILLER BAY RESIDENCE

Indianola, Washington — 1998

THE SITE OF THE MILLER BAY RESIDENCE is at the end of a sand spit in Puget Sound. It faces west across a narrow opening between Port Madison and Miller Bay and has views of Mount Rainier to the south. The site had a substantial grove of shore pines near where the house would be built, and this became a key element of the design. I decided to use the grove as a kind of gateway in the entry procession. Moving from the parking area to the house, a boardwalk leads through the pines toward the front door. I also determined that the house should be low slung, so as to not overwhelm the pine grove. Thus the landscape and the building form an architectural whole.

A handful of branches needed to be carefully pruned along the line of march in order to open a space for the entry arbor. This arbor establishes a threshold before the entrance. It also introduces a language of wood arbor structures used on both the east entry and the west terrace. After moving through the arbor, one passes through a low-ceilinged entry space to reach the great room and its view of the bay beyond.

Designed to accommodate wheelchair movement, the house and boardwalks sit exactly at grade. The plan of the house is roughly symmetrical, with bedroom wings arranged at each end of the high-ceilinged great room. The bedroom wings are slightly canted like bird wings, as if pushing the main volume forward toward the shore.

My clients came to me expressing an interest in the architecture of the prairie school and of Japan. The prairie style is referenced in the broad roof overhangs, which are intended to emphasize the plane of the beachfront site. I interpreted the house's wall and window elements—large panels of cedar shingles and glass—as abstractions inspired by the exteriors of the Katsura Imperial Villa in Kyoto. The glass window panels have long horizontal panes, both to emphasize the line of the water views beyond and to evoke the architecture of Japan.

I developed a material palette comprising a cedar shingle exterior, with native Wilkeson sandstone, quarried near Mount Rainier, for the massive symmetrical chimneys and the pergola supports. The interior is executed entirely in hemlock.

LEFT *Preliminary sketch of the landscape and building masses.*
BELOW *Concept study in watercolor.*

THIS PAGE *Schematic elevation showing the house's shore pine surroundings and site plan with solar diagram.* OPPOSITE *The entry pergola leads through the shore pine grove to the house, and thence to a terrace on the bay.*

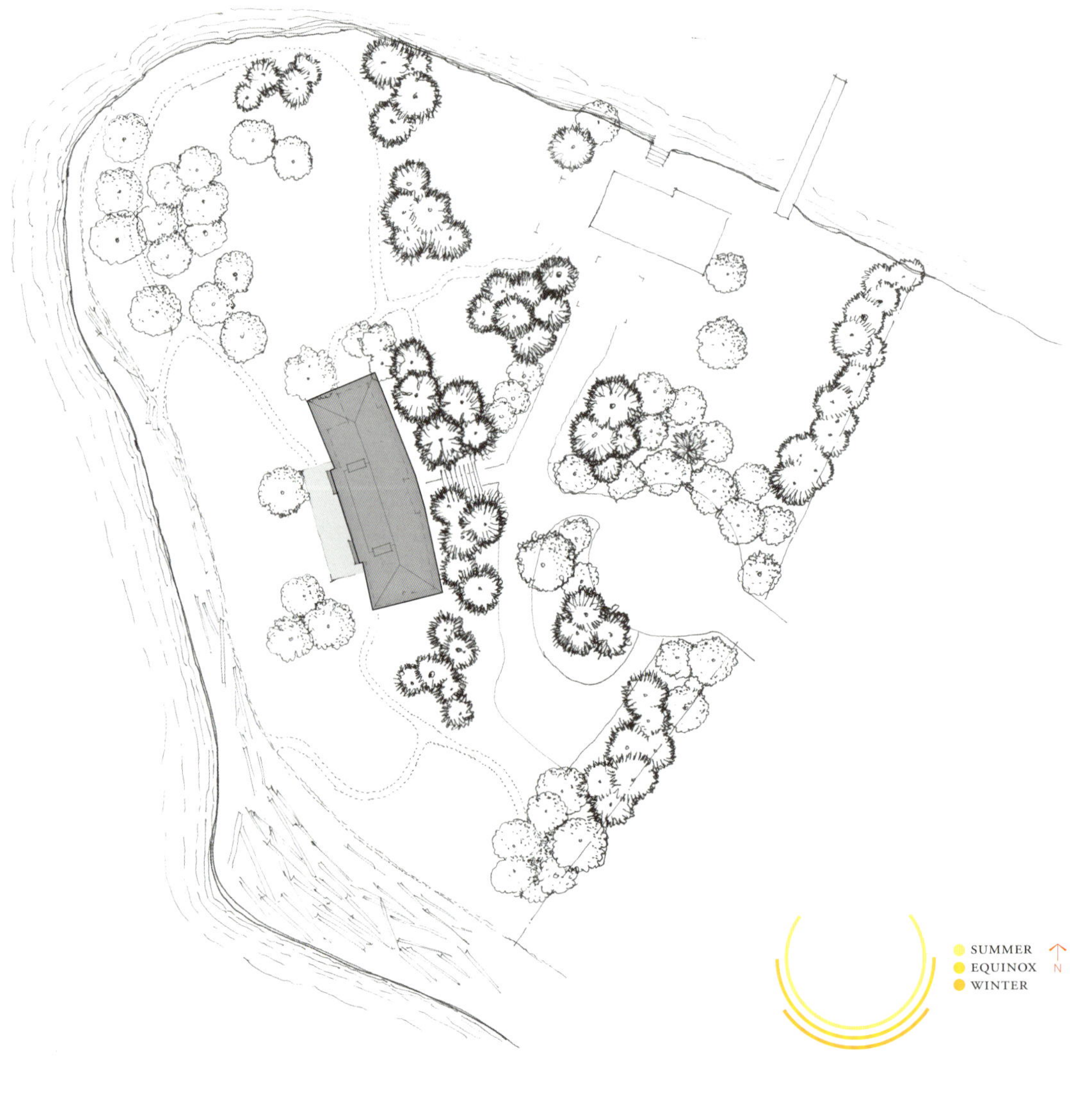

Schematic sketch of north elevation.

BELOW *Schematic site section, showing interior volumes and clerestory.*
OPPOSITE *The great room's steel trusses support its arched clerestory, which softens the exterior form.*

ORDER

Houses can be disorienting labyrinths of spaces that fail to orient users to the building and to their relationship with the site, or with the larger world. In my design process, I try to establish an ordering framework early on in order to guide the decision-making process that follows the initial concept. Determining the proportions of rooms (their width, length, and height) and organizing their geometric assembly, one with the other, in an efficient and natural progression on the site is where the design of the plan aligns with the site analysis. Rigor in this process enhances a clarity of intention.

The architects of the ancient classical world used symmetry to create a fundamental sense of order and orientation. James S. Ackerman stated in a lecture I attended on the architecture of Andrea Palladio that symmetry is the most memorable form of order. The axes of symmetry in ancient Greek temples were oriented to geologic points in the larger landscape, as these were experienced as sacred places. Using these axes to embed the building in the larger context of the land expressed the human relationship with what Vincent Scully called the "essential holiness of the land" in his book *The Earth, the Temples, and the Gods.*[4]

Symmetry introduces order and orientation to the larger world by means of the directional axis. It also introduces the concept of hierarchy, as the most important spaces are located closest to the axes of symmetry. In my work, I have often used symmetry as a starting point. In part this is the result of my background—my training in and interest in classical architecture, and my experience with the traditional architecture of the New England home of my youth. In part it is because symmetry is simply a ready ordering device. Symmetry may suggest itself as an organizing system on a large site, creating a spatial procession of entry along an axis. Or it may be used locally within a suite of rooms in order to create an internal sense of orientation.

Geometrical relationships—along with establishing hierarchical relationships of relative emphasis and importance—play a part in organizing the programmatic elements that seek expression in three-dimensional space. Here I find it helpful to consult history, and particularly the architects of the Italian Renaissance, in seeking the right proportions for a given space. Andrea Palladio's *The Four Books on Architecture* proposes a system of proportions based on the geometries of the square (1:1) and the golden rectangle (1:1.618). These proportions codify centuries of experience in Western art into a system of what makes a space *feel* right.

The Four Books on Architecture is, in a way, a treatise on geomancy, addressing similar attributes of spatial orientation as the arts of feng shui in China and vastu shastra in India. It seems to me that all of these geomantic arts aspire to encode an attitude of receptivity to the specific places where buildings seek to express themselves, in an authentic alignment with the natural forces held there.

An ordering system may possess overlays of order, as, for example, when the primary axis of a building is also the axis of solar orientation. This layering deepens the meaning of orientation by confirming spatial relationships to the sun. When I discover a natural overlay of multiple systems of order, I sense an inevitability emerge in the organization of building spaces. This tunes a building to both an intellectual system of order and the central point of order in our cosmos: the sun.

Katachi: *slab-built stoneware vessel, using impressed circular stamp pattern, with bronze-colored glaze fired in soda atmosphere.*

Another ordering system that has a prominent history in Western domestic architecture is the courtyard. The concentricity of the courtyard space was already well established in the Mediterranean world when the builders of Pompeii created atrium-centered houses. The Bronze Age Palace of Knossos, dating from the second millennium BCE, juxtaposes the spatial center of a courtyard with labyrinthian processional spaces surrounding it. The courtyard organizes all the myriad ancillary spaces around its central roofless core: the walled garden. The inhabitant has only to look toward the courtyard to know where they are, to know the time of day, and that they are in the relative safety of the private enclosure. Due to its prominence in the spatial hierarchy, it will be the important destination on a procession from the outer world into the inner familial world.

A sense of spatial orientation is important to a basic feeling of well-being. The human inner ear sends a continuous stream of signals to the brain; these convey the location of the head in space within a three-dimensional grid of *x*-, *y*-, and *z*-axes. This is our human positioning system, without which we have no sense of balance, no certainty of where we are.

Similarly, we seek information in our surroundings in order to understand our relationship to the spaces we move through and the spaces that we inhabit. A built environment that gives us a continuous stream of information about where we are within it provides a sense of orientation and, therefore, a sense of spatial security.

In my work, I like to think of ordering systems as necessary components in generating intelligibility. But if they are used with a relentless inviolability, they become lifeless formulas. Like the grain of sand in the birth of a pearl, some irritation, some internal conflict that refuses to submit to order, is, to me, welcome. Often, the piece that will not fit, that will not submit to the larger order, presents itself as an unresolvable problem. The rational mind cannot accept the inconsistency of such a piece. And yet that place of tension that the "problem" brings forth makes it possible to let go of rigid thinking and allows the pure scheme to deform in favor of the real demands of a site, or of a program, or of some other unplanned influence. Order cannot be perceived without the threat of chaos that such opportunities bring forward in the design process.

BLUE ATLAS RESIDENCE

Seattle, Washington — 2014

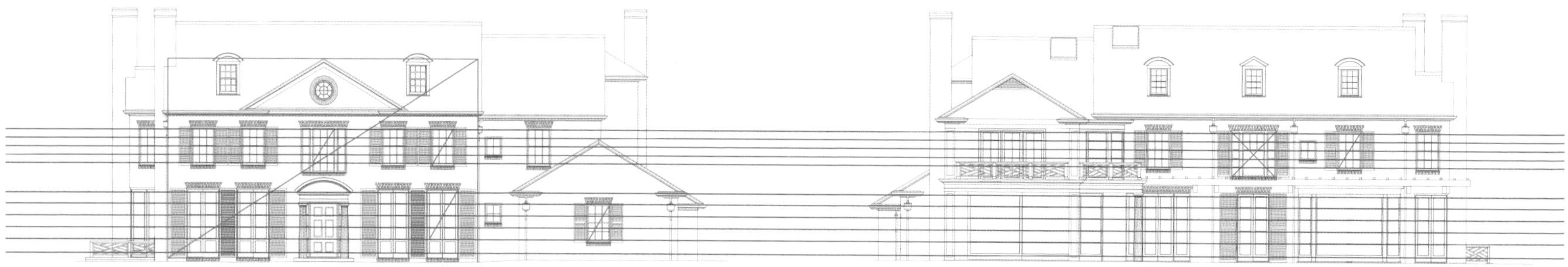

THE BLUE ATLAS RESIDENCE straddles the opposing worlds of public versus private and classical versus modern. The clients wished to build a home that referenced the historic style of Georgian England and at the same time used contemporary expanses of glass fenestration to connect to a large garden. This starting point presented a conflict—a seemingly contradictory request to merge classical order with modern elements. My approach was to create a classical front to the house, guided by neoclassical principles, and a glassy garden facade in a spirit of open transparency.

I used ordering principles of classical architecture to establish the proportions of the entire structure. This classical language regulates the proportions of the main facades as well as the windows. The front facade is a five-bay pedimented composition, a favorite of both Georgian England and the Italian Renaissance. This is the public front: well mannered, reserved, embracing ancient traditions. Classical ordering translates from this main entry facade and the formal spaces into the greater openness, informality, and modernism of the garden facades. This is the private front: undefended, open, and seeking contact with the natural world.

As an example of the process that I used to establish the primary architectural order, the front facade displays a classical pediment to connote its hierarchical primacy. The pediment is conceived as a floating triangle that sits at the centerline of the cornice. To determine the size of the pediment as an element of the total composition, I used regulating lines and the golden section, the classic 1:1.618 ratio. The height of the pediment is determined by using the width of the central block of the building as the long side of a golden rectangle, and the short side as the height of the facade plus its pediment (that is, the height of the implied rectangle of the entire facade). This created a pediment that sits with some tension (by strict classical standards) on the wall below relative to its window openings. A continuous cornice allows for a solid base for the triangle of the pediment, anchoring it in the composition.

This is an intuitive compositional approach to classical elements, instead of an attempt for something more canonical. This approach was essential, given the design explorations—the merging of both classical and modern architectural languages—that this building embodies. Abstracting differing architectural languages to their elemental forms allows for this transliteration of style.

Another example of compositional freedom within established guidelines is the ordering of windows on the entry facade. I arranged and proportioned most of the windows according to classical principles. However, I exaggerated the scale of the first floor French windows in order to create large openings. The tops of these windows reach to the ceiling, without using a visible structural header at the interior. This allows natural light to rake across the ceiling, enhancing natural daylight illumination in the spare light of the Pacific Northwest. Enlarging the French windows also introduces a scale shift from the traditional window proportions to the contemporary expansive fenestration on the garden facade. The horizontal muntins in the classically proportioned windows at the entry align with the full-height contemporary sliding glass walls on the garden, unifying these two languages by means of a common geometry.

Pleasing proportional relationships elicit associations in the human mind of balance, of feeling right. The same can be said of elements of scale, at the

OPPOSITE *Regulating lines show the use of golden rectangles and squares to compose the facade.*
BELOW *Preliminary sketches of entry and garden elevations.*

finer level of the craft of building. Take, for example, the forms of windows and doors. The mullions and the muntins of a window wall system establish a detailed relationship with the human body and, therefore, the body's understanding of how it correlates in size to its surroundings. It is curious to me that the size of a pane of glass in traditional architecture was roughly the size of a human head. In Georgian England and in early colonial buildings in America, the pane of glass was most often proportioned to the golden rectangle. And so, encoded in the fenestration (the eyes of the building) was the scale of the human figure. By amplifying or reducing the proportions of windows, architects can make a building feel relatively larger or smaller compared to the scale of the human body.

The use of large expanses of glass on the garden side of the Blue Atlas Residence enhances the visual connection between inside and outside spaces, diminishing boundaries of separation from the landscape. Yet it may also diminish the sense of the human scale and texture, resulting in a more abstract reading of the building. The careful crafting of these proportional elements creates a formal language with which a building engages with its particular site.

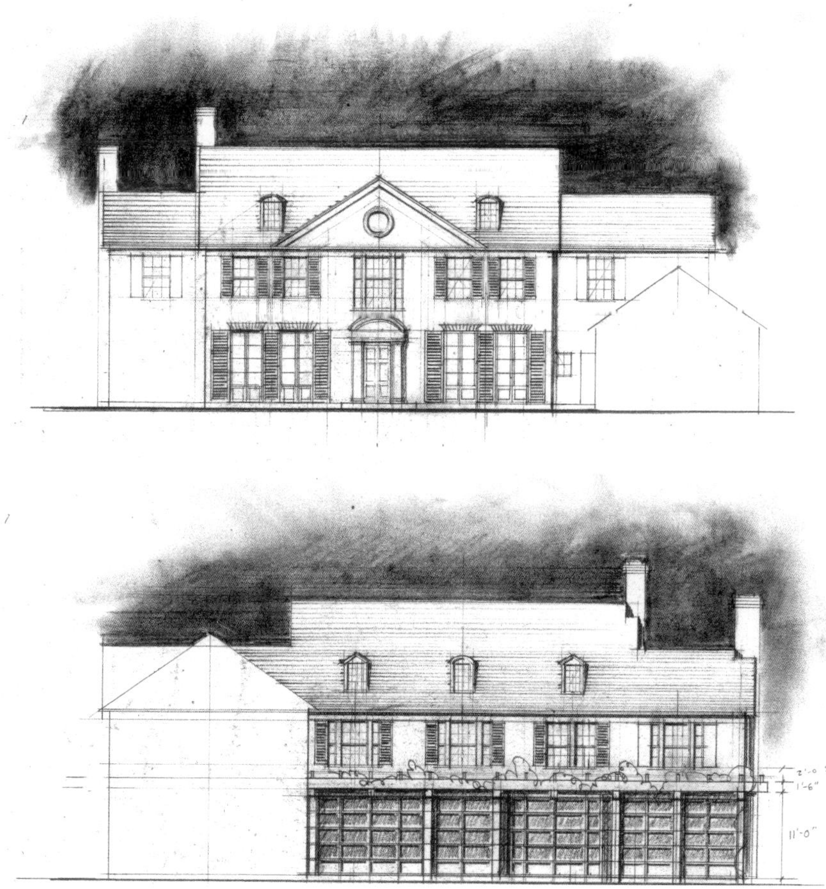

OPPOSITE *The rear elevation shows the transition between the classical language of the main volume and the more contemporary fenestration of the garden side.*
BELOW *Site plan showing garden setting and solar diagram.*

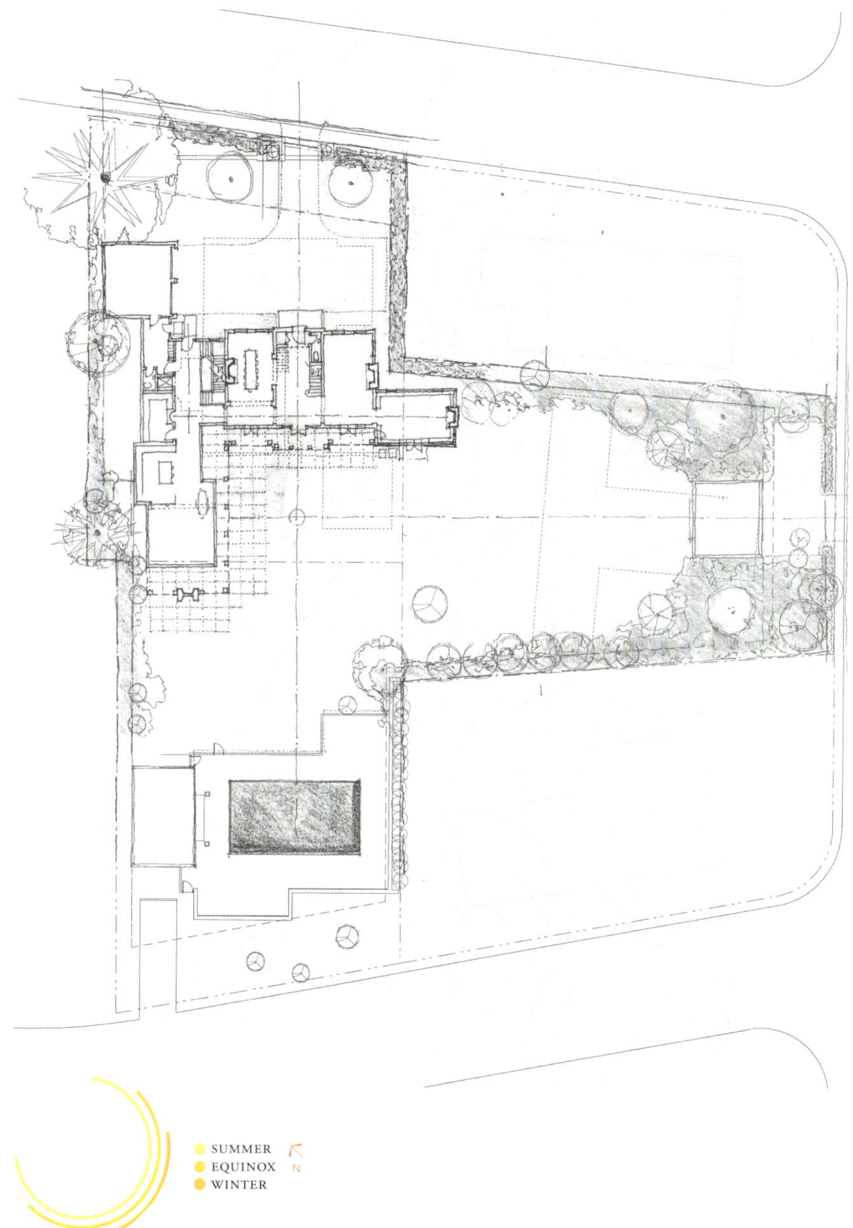

BELOW *Detailed drawings of the arched pediment and the entablature of the entry porch.*
RIGHT *The family room wing at dusk.*

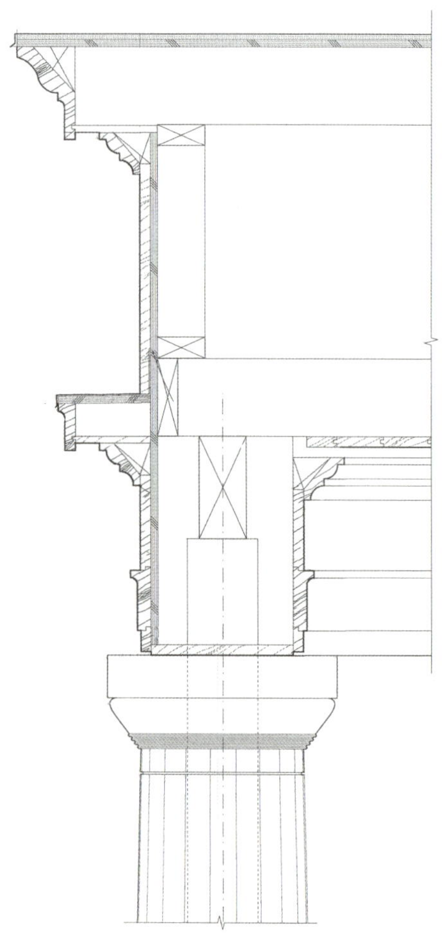

The sliding window walls of the living and family rooms on the garden side are large expanses of horizontal glass panes.

The full-height windows on the garden side illuminate the ceiling with the low-raking light of the Pacific Northwest.

BOTANICALS

The stair hall displays the simplified classical detailing that characterizes the interior.

ASGARD RESIDENCE

Medina, Washington — 1999

THE ASGARD RESIDENCE DESIGN is founded in classical ordering systems of symmetry and strict proportional relationships. The husband of the client couple is European, and the wife is a native of the Pacific Northwest. Each brought their memories of the feeling of home forward in our design collaboration. He loves classicism and is passionate about the opera. She loves the quality of the light of her native region and welcomes as much of it as possible into interior spaces.

My design effort was to balance classical order and restraint with an exuberant connection to light and views of an adjacent lake. The dialog between the clients, regarding his love of classicism and her love of the spatial connection with the site and the desire for light, informed the design. The house resolves the inherent tension between the ordering principles of classicism and the unique qualities of its lakefront site.

The large lakefront site includes a long access drive. A slight meander in this road and the planting of new trees heighten the sense of anticipation of arrival at a stone-paved courtyard. The house is positioned northward on the site so as to maximize a south garden and to bring southern light into the house.

Upon arrival at the car court, a central entry porch, trimmed with limestone and inscribed with the name *Asgard*, claims the central axis. The name connotes a divine realm, a Norse place of heavenly dwelling. In plan, the classically inflected U-shaped shell of the more public elevations surrounds on three sides a grand two-storied great room containing the main living area. Responding to the clients' love of opera, the house has the feeling of a stage and this great room is its proscenium. It faces the lakefront toward the Olympic Peninsula on the western horizon. A sequence of terrace spaces leads from this great room down to the beachfront and swimming pool. Multiple roof terraces offer connections to the outdoors from the upper level.

A material palette of stucco, limestone, and slate roof tiles conveys the relative solidity of traditional European building construction. This palette is used for the front and the sides of the structure. In contrast, the lakefront facade gives way to a two-story window wall of wood and glass, with French doors opening to the terrace and the lakeside pool.

Departing from the imagery of the classical, a broad roof with substantial overhangs exaggerates the horizontality of the scheme on the lakefront facade. The roof is punctuated by symmetrically placed chimney masses that bookend the great room.

BELOW *Concept scheme showing the spatial procession through the site.*
RIGHT *Site plan with solar diagram.*

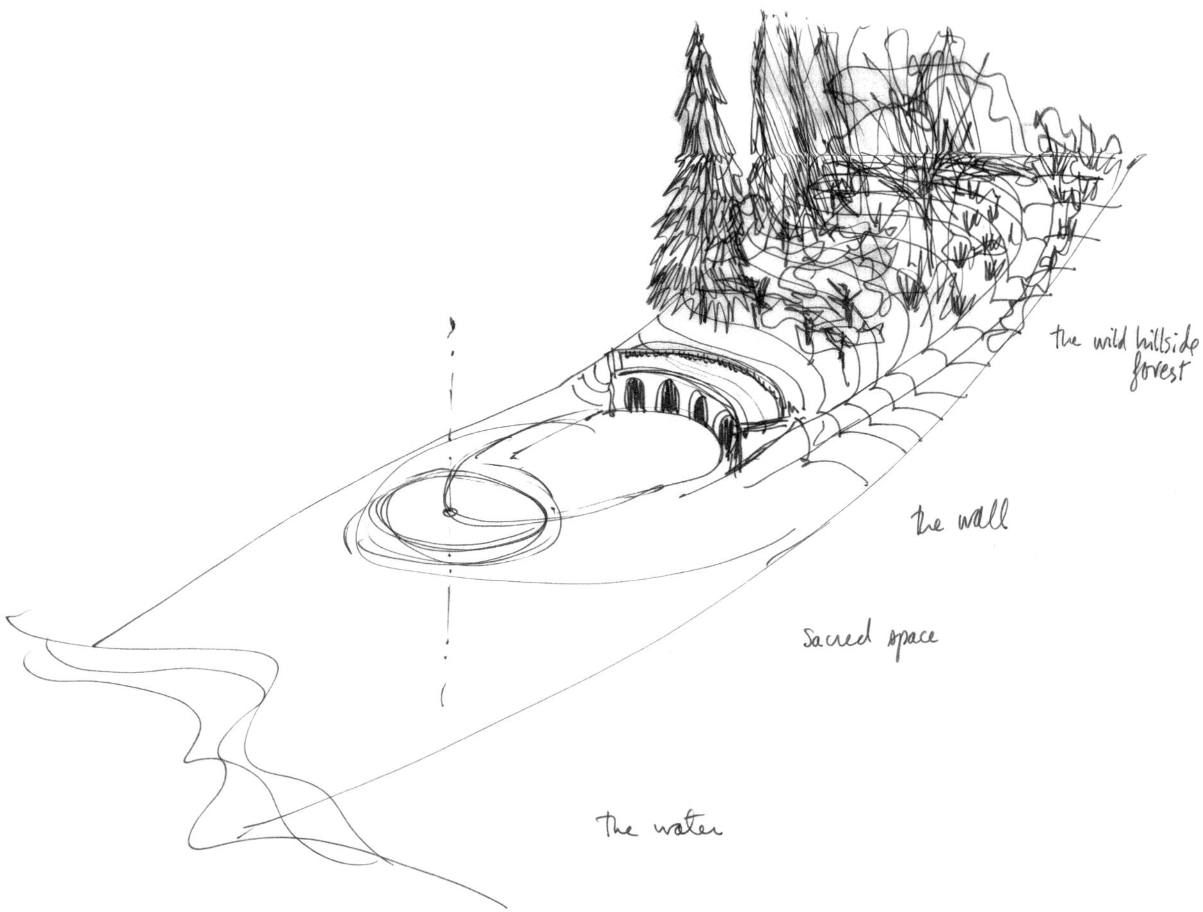

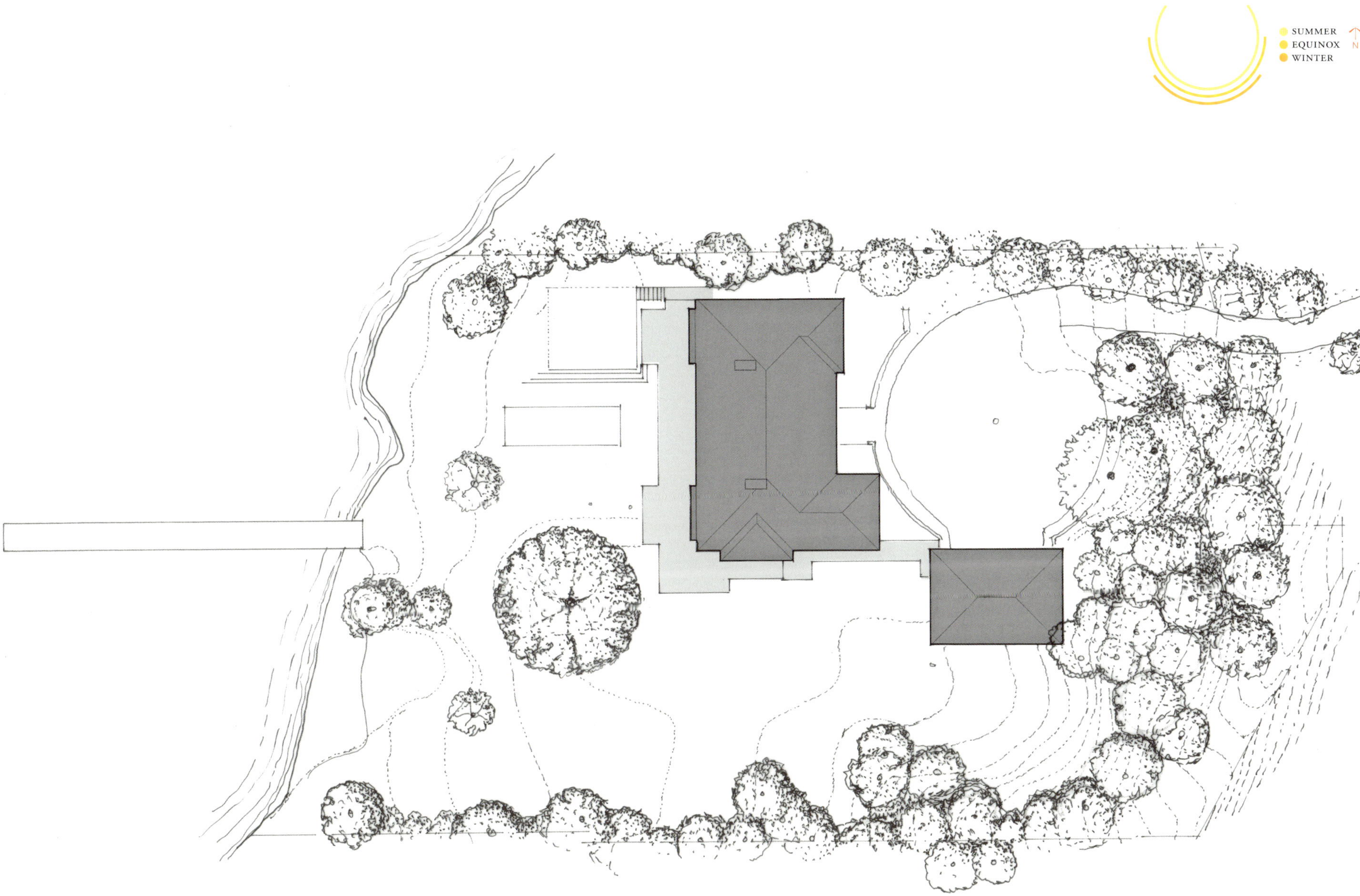
SUMMER
EQUINOX
WINTER
N

STEPHEN SULLIVAN

LEFT *Sketches of the entry facade, showing development of the massing and detailing.*
RIGHT *The entry portico showing Doric pilaster capitals, entablature, and cornice in limestone.*

RIGHT *The house has the feeling of a stage with this great room as its proscenium.*
OPPOSITE *The stairway leads to a balcony suspended over the main living space.*

NARRATIVE

THE HOUSES THAT I DESIGN start out as abstractions—as spatial diagrams and spatial sequences—informed in their composition by the intentional considerations of the orientation of each space to the larger context of site. I could imagine a way of designing architecture that ends with the abstract diagram. Greater volumes hold the most important spaces, larger windows open the most public spaces to the outdoors, smaller windows let in light to the more private spaces, and roof overhangs control the sun's heat with shade. The design emerges as an abstract expression of the program.

But abstractions can express only so much. As mythologist Michael Meade wrote, "As human beings, we live and we die in the context of the stories we tell about ourselves, about the world and our place in it."[5] The Parthenon in Athens held stories in its pediments, carved in stone, about its founding goddess, Athena, and about battles and conflicts that gave birth to the city and its culture. The pottery of the Greeks, Etruscans, and Romans likewise celebrates cultural myths and stories, reminding the users of the sources of their very lives. The surfaces of Gothic cathedrals are dense with biblical instruction. What messages do we receive from our contemporary buildings about who we are and who we aspire to be, both as individuals and as a culture in this time?

I was trained in a mode of design analysis, in a kind of functional modernism, that elevated early twentieth-century Bauhaus architecture to the pediment of honor. It seems to me that the story told by this type of modernism was the elevation of the machine (Le Corbusier's "A house is a machine for living in") and the rejection of historic reference. It is not surprising that this wholesale rejection of past traditions of building followed two devastating wars in Europe, with their nationalist overtones. The very term International Style, attributed to the school of European modernism, suggests the rejection of Europe's prewar dysfunctional self-image. The International Style holds in its message the rejection of the past and of the vernacular, and the looking toward a new vision of society.

However, this vision of architecture as a machine seemed limited to me, especially after apprenticing in postwar Japan as a potter in the folk-craft *(mingei)* tradition. There I learned that the handcrafted object, intended for daily use, was a revered cultural expression, especially in the face of the rampant industrialization in the twentieth century. The beautifully crafted item was indeed an antidote to the impersonality of mechanized society, and 1920s-era Japan had given birth to an aesthetic movement to honor and to revive the dying traditions of its crafts.

The custom home is a crafted object. In my practice, working with the best craftspeople in a community in order to execute a building of the highest quality is a collaboration and a profound honor. Woodworkers, stone masons, metal craftspeople, artisans, and artists come together to create a home. I have witnessed many times a kind of competitive spirit when these artists show with pride their great efforts of expression in their craft, each inspired by the others to execute at the highest level they can achieve. The elevation of craft is an important part of the narrative that I seek in my design work. Why, in this time of mechanization and digitization, will a person decide to work with their hands in a material they love to touch?

The choice and refinement of a material palette in my design work is fundamental. Wood, stone, brick, concrete, and glass all have their particular

Sensei: *slab-built stoneware vessel with rope-impressed inlay of pigmented slips and photo silk-screened image, fired in soda atmosphere.*

histories and associations with place and with a period in time. The decision to build a house that expresses wood craftsmanship for a Pacific Northwest family whose business is in the timber industry is a natural expression of place. Electing to use board-formed concrete for the construction of a house designed as a series of planted hillside terraces is intended as an expression of the geologic layers of the hillside itself. The board forms mimic the geologic layers at the fine scale, while the cantilevered terraces mimic the larger scale of the stepping hillside.

Buildings of stone or fired-clay bricks connote substantiality and permanence. These material choices engage the senses, especially at those points of direct human contact with the building, such as a hand rail or door handle. There are cultural messages as well as personal associations contained in materials. To build a house of brick in the Pacific Northwest necessarily carries associations with the history of East Coast cities or Georgian London. And what story does a house made from stones hauled out of the Yangtze in China tell, if not the story of twentieth-century global trade?

When I was engaged to design a house in the Sonoran Desert of Arizona, the community's homeowners' association required that I define my design within their specific taxonomy of allowable styles. It was obvious that the design did not conform to any of the condoned types defined by this community (which had made-up names such as "Santa Barbara Mission Style"). I submitted the plans under the most generic term—Southwest Contemporary—yet even this nonsense "style" had specific requirements to which the design did not conform. While this community's struggle to define appropriate style, so as to encode a community-wide agreement about what constituted architectural quality, was well intentioned, it laid the foundations for stylistic pastiche as opposed to good architecture.

The community's own best intentions were foiled by placing emphasis on the most superficial aspects of historic reference as a starting point of design, instead of encouraging a specific creative response to the environment of a place, with its unique desert flora, geology, and topography. In its view, the overlay of historic reference was more important than an authentic response to the place itself. The group sought to invoke fake styles instead of creating guidelines to make an architecture embedded in the unique nature of the place.

The stories contained in design, such as the choice of materials, build in layers that start with a client's personal associations. At this level, the stories hold a psychological resonance with connections from the past, or a sense of belonging or comfort. Architects and clients may choose materials out of respect for a regional expression of geology, as in the Southwest, or forestry, as in the Pacific Northwest. Such site-specific choices invoke a foundational aspect of the place or a region. They may also hold larger historical references. Each layer conveys meaning, and these layers of meaning build upon each other in a palimpsest to tell both a personal story and a story of place.

MERCER ISLAND RESIDENCE

Mercer Island, Washington — 2001

BELOW *Schematic sketch of south entry.*
OPPOSITE *The entry court is paved with antique granite cobbles from China's Yangtze River Valley.*

OVER THE YEARS, several clients have come to me seeking houses that express the traditions of the East Coast, and in particular the shingle style of the coastal Northeast. Given the fir- and cedar-forested rocky coastline of Washington State, with imaginings of summers by the sea, shingle-clad houses seem to me a natural expression of the place.

The shingle style evolved in the atmosphere of the Gilded Age of the late nineteenth and early twentieth century. At that time the saltbox—the prototypical New England house type—could no longer hold the expressive ambitions of pre–income tax wealth generated in the post–Civil War economic expansion. A house type, especially for summer houses, that was large and sprawling and graced with ample porches evolved during that period. The cubically contained shingled saltbox of the past gave way to a rambling picturesque architecture. Its taught shingled skin was the same as that of the historic saltbox, and its classical symmetries and articulation of detail were similar, but it was relatively palatial in comparison to the old prototype.

The Mercer Island Residence represents a group of shingle-clad houses that I have designed. All are on the shores of the Puget Sound, with sloping sites. To address the slopes, I designed long terraces at the water sides, connecting the primary rooms to the view and to each other. The plan of each is symmetrical, in the sense that it has a strong central core with wings to each side.

This house on Mercer Island commands a promontory on a site sloping north to Lake Washington with views of the lake. A long driveway, cobbled in antique granite and lined with an allée of birch trees designed by landscape

Watercolor rendering of the lakefront facade.

architect Richard Haag, leads to the entry court. The slope required that the house sit on a terraced plinth, also paved with granite. The entry sequence from the driveway steps down a short flight of curved steps to an intimate entry court and on to a glassy south-facing main entry.

The plan centers on the axial entry, celebrated with its southern window bay and punctuated with a pedimented roof. The exterior skin is shingled, and I used a classical order of columns and pilasters to articulate porches, the lakefront trellis, and secondary details.

The entry stair hall is also classically detailed, and it leads to the columned central bay of the main room. This room combines the formal living and dining spaces with the central axis in a tripartite plan. It holds the central position in the plan and leads to a terrace overlooking the lake. A spacious pine-paneled library wing, with its large apsidal porch, counterbalances the high-volumed informal family room and kitchen wing. A guest space and pool cabana are conceived as a kind of grotto, partially embedded below the family terrace and leading to a lower pool terrace.

LEFT *A classical order of columns and pilasters articulates porches, the trellis, and secondary details.* BELOW *Preliminary sketch of the lakefront facade and site plan with solar diagram.*

The entry hall leads to the columned central bay of the main room.

LEFT *A view to a pine-paneled library beyond the fireplace.*
BELOW *The kitchen wing.*

The pine-paneled library opens out to the apsidal porch.

INTEGRATION

Renga: *slab-built stoneware vessel of Shigaraki clay, rope impressed with iron slip inlay, fired in the yohen wood ash chamber of the Shimaoka noborigama in Mashiko, Japan.*

In my work, there has never been a straight line from the inception of a design to that moment when it all comes together, and the disparate layers finally add up to something that resonates as true. The integration of the site and energy analyses, with a system of order that gives form to the initial concepts, requires patience, perseverance, and a willingness to let go, time and time again, of ideas that are too small to grasp the larger complexity that seeks expression in a building.

I was first introduced to the idea of letting go as a young potter in a traditional apprenticeship in Japan. At that time, apprentices like me might be required to copy the same cup shape, over and over again, all day long, seven days a week, for months without interruption. Our cups would be periodically inspected by the master, and most, if not all, would be recycled in the clay bin because they were not correct in form, or in weight, or in the execution of the foot or the rim. The goal in this process was to teach us to not be attached to the object, while steadfastly aiming toward the true form.

For an American in his early twenties, experiencing this concentrated focus was, at times, extremely difficult. While I was given some slack for being a *gaijin* (foreigner), I still held myself to the standards I witnessed around me. A diligent work ethic, communal effort, the silent communication of how to make a well-crafted object, and precisely timed tea breaks filled my days for a year in Japan. We worked solely with local materials; thus our pots were the result of the very earth of the local hills around us.

Working in this way, I learned to be detached from a specific outcome of my productivity and to be immersed in an unceasing process of refinement. This eventually led me toward a greater sureness of gesture that was based in bodily memory rather than willful effort. I had travelled to Japan imagining that I would learn much about the ceramic arts of that country. But the lessons that were the most important were not the ones that I had expected to learn. Watching other potters enter into a state of self-abandonment and creative flow was the most significant lesson.

As an architect, I reflect on this reiterative process, like making 1,000 cups of the same form. In my design studio, I still work in the old way of unrolling tracing paper over a design sketch in order to best perceive the refinements that are called for in the vison for an emerging story. In a way, this method of design reiteration is parallel to the act of throwing at the potter's wheel, over and over, until there is an unselfconscious flow and a truer form, characterized by simplicity and efficiency, emerges. By means of this process of reiteration, it is possible to reduce the visual noise of the roughly sculpted form, eliminating the unnecessary and abstracting the essential qualities of a design. By minimizing distracting variations within a design theme, the object moves toward an inevitable simplicity.

At the same time, there will remain those elements that do not quite fit, that cause irritation. I recall Gerhard Kallmann, my professor at Harvard, criticizing a student's design project during a final review. He commended the work while also asking, "But where is the door for the tiger?" I gather that his comment was a reference to something that Alvar Aalto had said regarding making room for an essential wildness in the midst of refinement and order. Tadao Ando makes a similar argument for "imperfection" when he states, "In architecture, there is a part that is the result of logical reasoning and a part that is created through the senses. There is always a point where they clash. I don't think architecture can be created without that collision."[6]

CLIFF RESIDENCE

San Juan Islands, Washington — 2012

BELOW *A wall of sliding windows opens the main space to the bay.*
OPPOSITE *The chimney is formed of glacial granite hauled from a neighboring site on barges.*

OFF THE COAST OF WASHINGTON STATE, the San Juan Islands are characterized by a landscape of glacially carved granite and basalt outcrop islands covered in lush moss-bedded forests of evergreen Douglas fir and western red cedar trees. I have lived in the Pacific Northwest for nearly half a century, drawn here by its natural beauty. The San Juan Islands have been both a spiritual home and an actual home for me. The unique qualities of the coastal rock forms and the native forests of cedar and fir hold me as only a well-known landscape can. Thus many of the decisions about how to build in this place seem almost preordained, as if the site were simply expressing itself in the form of human shelter.

My clients for the Cliff Residence had a family compound in the San Juan Islands, and they planned to expand the compound to include a new house for family members. I met with them on several occasions to walk the site, topographic surveys in hand, in order to evaluate the exact siting of the proposed structure. We spent many hours together studying nuances in the rock forms—nobs, outlooks, and ravines. They had intimate knowledge of the rock cliff, its moss meadows, and individual mature trees, and they intended to impart this knowledge to me as we imagined the new house. We searched for the right topographic bench on the sloping site on which to embed the building. The final siting required that we blast into bedrock on the uphill side and create a stone terrace on the downhill south side, looking out over the bay.

left *The slope of the roof mimics that of the topography so as to embed the building in its site.*
right *Preliminary concept sketch.*

The family had built earlier structures with a material palette of fir timbers, cedar shingles, and local glacial fieldstone on the compound. These earlier buildings had taken some inspiration from the late-nineteenth-century Pasadena architectural firm Greene and Greene, whose house designs are known for their expressive use of furniture-like timber frames and deep roof overhangs. We agreed that the new buildings would honor this tradition.

The plan of the house has a south-facing great room with a large expanse of sliding window walls that engage a long stone terrace. Bedroom wings are placed symmetrically on each end of the great room. The terrace, and a pair of massive chimneys that bookend the volume of the great room, were constructed of native fieldstones culled from a neighboring island. Residents enter and leave the house through the great room via the stone terrace. In the benign climate of the Pacific Northwest, the room's large sliding window walls, reminiscent of Japanese shoji panels, can be left open during the day, allowing the great room to become a large-roofed volume open entirely to the sun-facing terrace and the bay beyond.

The house's timber frame is crafted as furniture, in the tradition of Greene and Greene and the craftsman style. Its stone is laid up with large boulders at the base and smaller stones as the walls and chimneys rise. The windows are proportioned as golden rectangles, large in scale and with heavy mullions, which add texture to the large expanses of glass. The landscapes are the forests and mossy outcrops from which the houses spring.

BELOW *View from the water showing the form of the roof as it relates to the slope of the cliff.*
RIGHT *Fieldstone terrace walls anchor the building to bedrock, while the Douglas fir structure honors the forest setting.*

BELOW *Site plan with solar diagram.*
OPPOSITE *The timber frame structure creates a deep overhang at the terrace.*

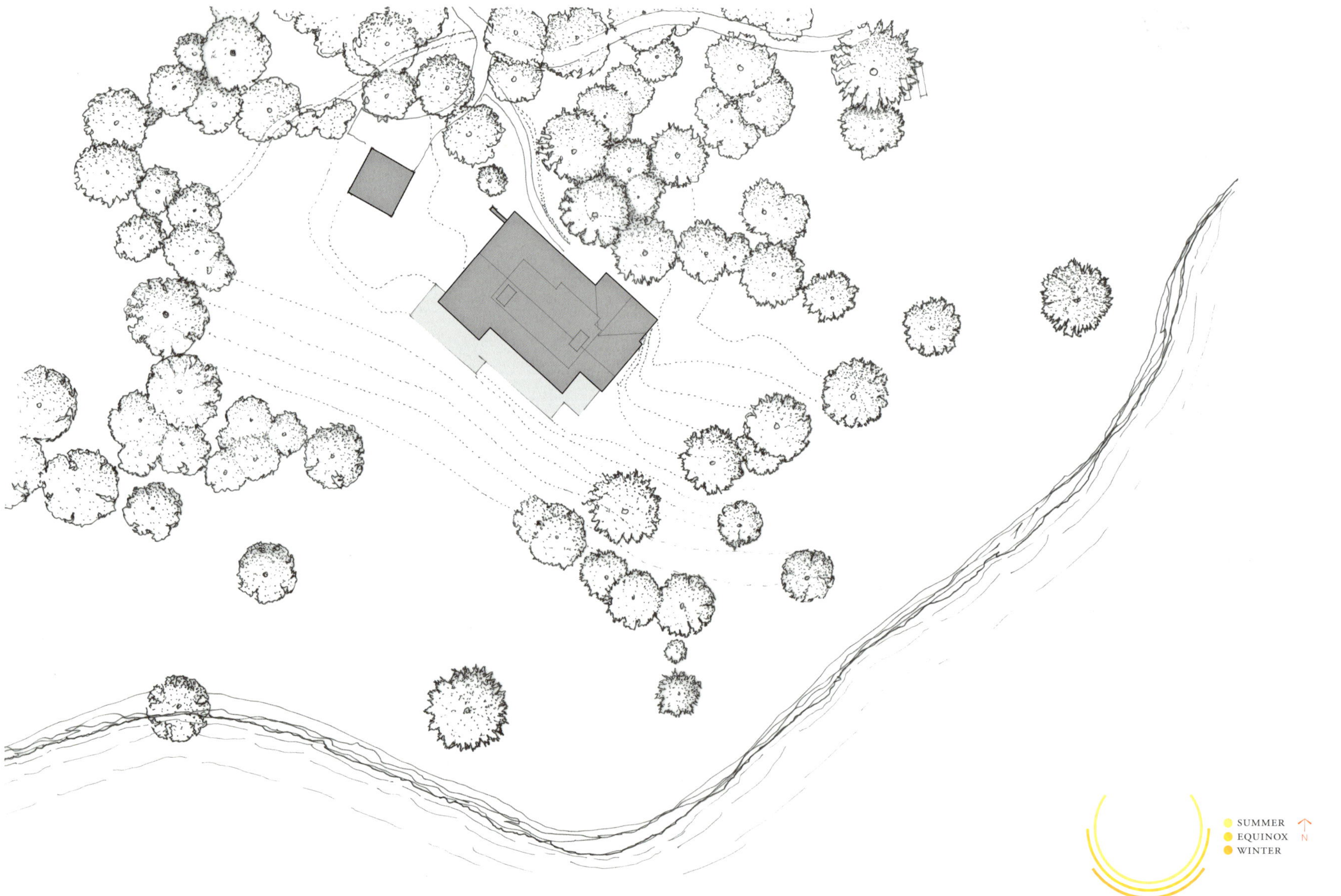

BELOW *Interior view showing embedment of building in its site.*
RIGHT *With a window wall open, the main room becomes a large roofed volume open to the terrace and the bay beyond.*
OVERLEAF *The Beach Residence is a fraternal twin of the Cliff Residence and sits on a low bank on the bay to the north.*

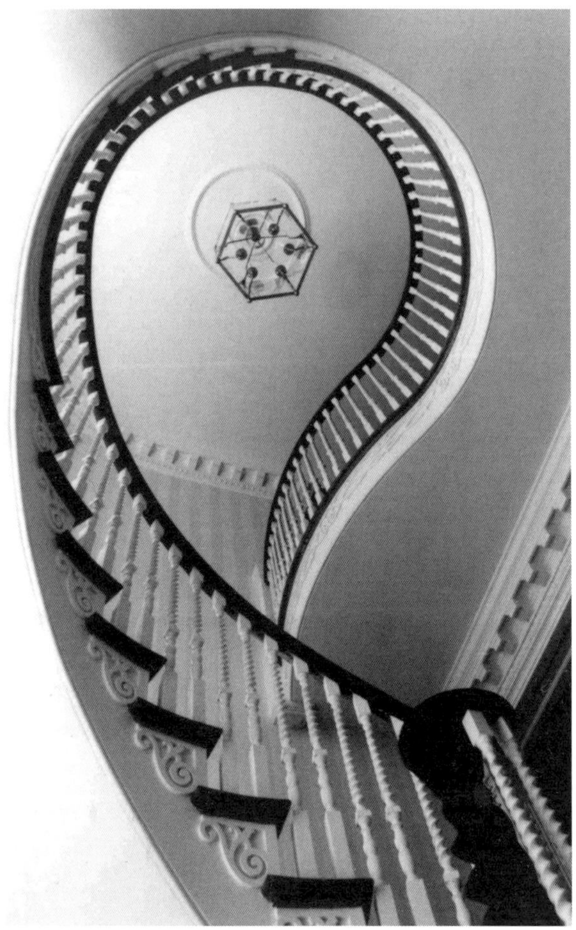

HISTORIC STRUCTURES

THE PROJECTS SHOWN HERE represent examples of my work on historic structures. Restoring, renovating, and making additions to venerable buildings requires restraint and respect for the original architecture. While some projects offer the possibility of episodic stylistic intervention, others, due to their protected status, require strict observation of the principles of true historic preservation.

Each of these projects holds significance to me as an architect. The main house at Lightning Tree Farm is a fine example of nineteenth-century classical revival architecture in the Hudson Valley of New York. My work there marked the beginning of my independent practice, thanks to the trust my clients, Libet Johnson and John Teal, offered to a young architect. The Lookout Residence is an example of Seattle's nod to East Coast colonial revival architecture in the early twentieth century. Executed decades after the Lightning Tree project, it was initiated at a time when I was transforming my architectural practice from a larger partnership to a more focused and smaller design studio, in collaboration with long-time clients. The Merrill Pergola and Carriage House, originally designed by Charles A. Platt of New York and built in 1909, is listed as a protected historic structure by the Seattle Landmarks Preservation Board. This project brought me back to my early interest in Platt as a high school student, and gave me the opportunity to give back to this important mentor by providing an invisible hand.

LIGHTNING TREE FARM RESIDENCE

Millbrook, New York — 1989

THE ORIGINAL MID-NINETEENTH-CENTURY residence at Lightning Tree Farm was a classical revival farmhouse. In the early twentieth century, a pair of symmetrical pavilions were added, flanking the pedimented entry front on the east side, facing the road.

In 1985, I was asked to design an addition to the residence's west side. The new facade formally addresses a spacious pastoral setting of farmland and stables, maintaining the axial tripartite scheme of the original structure. The intention of the design was to substantially enlarge the footprint to make room for a growing family. The wife of the client couple had an expansive vision of a country retreat for an active family, with equestrian stables for trail riding and a polo team, as well as agricultural operations.

The new plan expands the entry hall sequence from the public front to the back garden terrace, and introduces a highly detailed central staircase. The original house was distinguished by a formal Palladian geometry. I adapted the detail language of the classical architecture to the amplified scale of the new west facade, with its heroic order of pilasters framing the center bay. A new oval oculus window in the attic pediment and an arched window at the stair landing anchor the central axis of the composition.

Working with landscape architect Edwin Bye, I reshaped the entry drive into a large ellipse that enters through a park setting of mature trees to the front porch. A large stone terrace runs along the west facade, connecting the new library, entry hall, and family kitchen to the larger landscape. The interior architectural detailing of woodwork and plaster, designed in coordination with the interior designer David Easton, is based in the classical language.

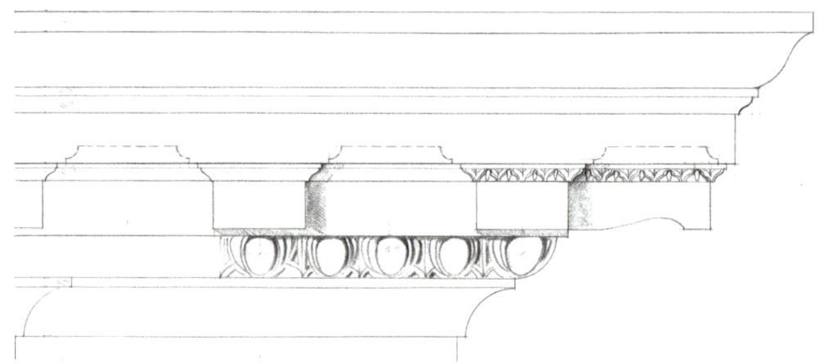

Design for the ceiling cornice of the entry stair hall.

OPPOSITE *The central arched window of the new rear addition looks out from the stair landing toward a pastoral landscape.*

RIGHT *A preliminary sketch shows the role of the central arched window.*
OPPOSITE *The new stair hall accommodates a circular stair with hand-carved, rope-turned balusters and scrolled fretwork.*

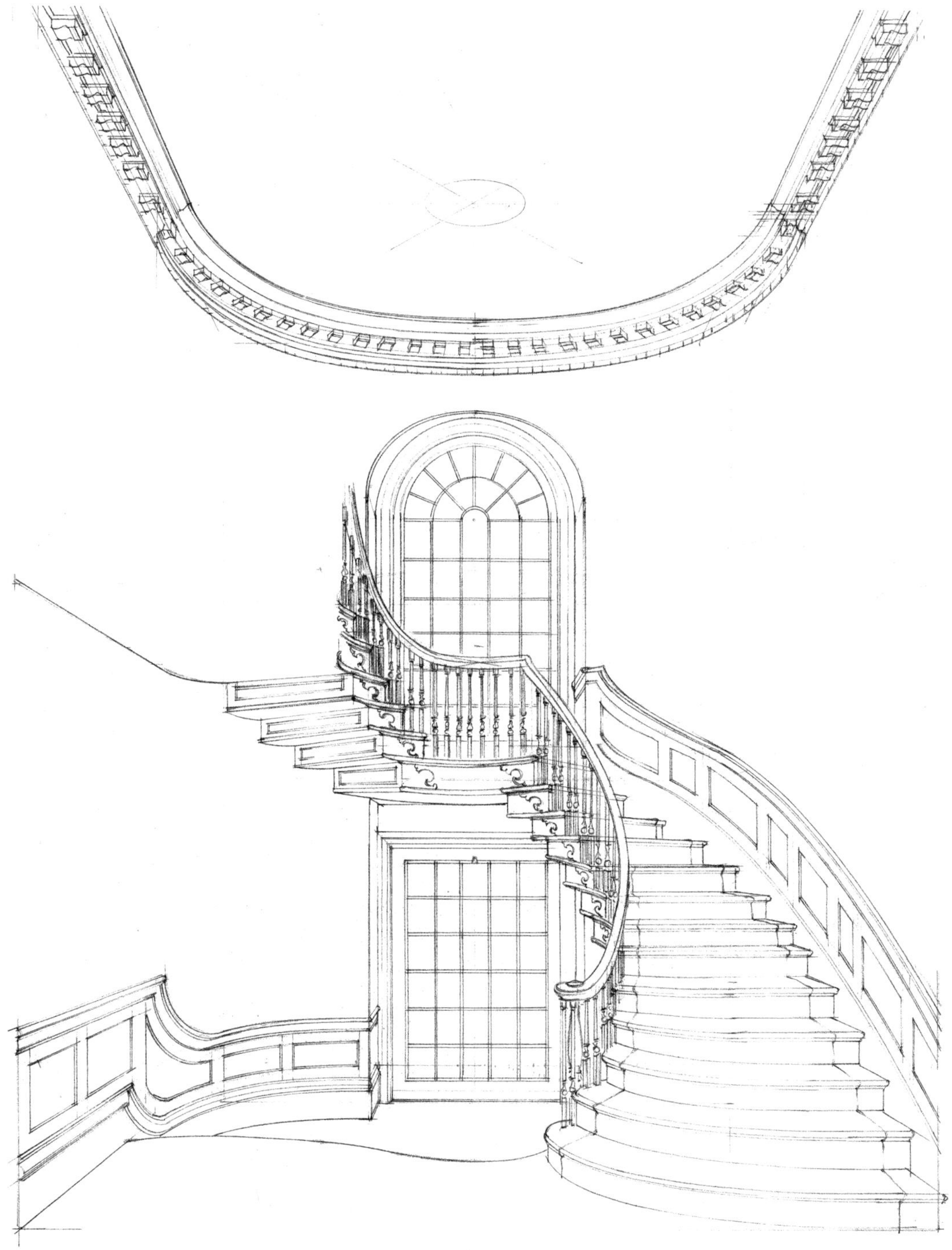

THE LOOKOUT RESIDENCE

Seattle, Washington — 2015

THE LOOKOUT RESIDENCE was originally built in the 1920s on a site with dramatic views of Lake Washington, the Cascade Range, and Mount Rainier. Set on a promontory high above the lake, the house meanders along its topographic shelf, with an enfilade of living spaces that open to the view.

The design team intended to preserve the integrity of the original by means of careful attention to the massing of elements and a sympathetic use of details. The basic plan of the residence was maintained, and a new garage wing, with a guest apartment above, and a new kitchen and family wing were added. An exception to the classical language of the original was introduced in the family room by means of steel sash doors and windows intended to maximize the sense of connection to the outdoors. A new series of terraces, both covered and open, create a spacious sequence of exterior spaces for entertaining and for engaging the gardens developed by landscape designers Glenn Withey and Charles Price.

OPPOSITE *A large terrace with bracket supports and glass roof expands the outdoor living area.*
BELOW *The entry court is conceived as a semiprivate garden.*

LEFT TOP *The dining room has walls of hand-cast mirrored glass.*
LEFT BOTTOM *The library took form within a former sun room.*
RIGHT *The new family room has steel stash windows and doors that look out over the lake.*

MERRILL PERGOLA AND CARRIAGE HOUSE

Seattle, Washington — 2021

THE ORIGINAL MERRILL PERGOLA was designed in 1909 by New York architect Charles A. Platt. Its cast-in-place concrete structure had fallen into disrepair and had suffered significant water intrusion over more than a century. Additionally, the building was in need of substantial structural reinforcement in order to carry the weight of a new sculpture that was to be displayed in it. The sculpture, a two-ton cast bronze piece by German sculptor Katharina Fritsch, creates a point load in the middle of the carriage house ceiling below. A new steel armature carries this load into the concrete bearing walls of the structure.

The finely cast cement details of the original building were sandblasted, removing layers of non-original paint, and restored to their natural concrete color. The pergola roof was rebuilt using Platt's original drawings for the detailing of wood "outriggers." The doors and windows were rebuilt using original hardware and, where possible, the original glass.

LEFT *Original hardware was copied and newly hand cast.*
BELOW *View of carriage house interior before restoration.*
OPPOSITE *The building was reinforced with a structural steel armature to carry the load of a cast bronze sculpture by artist Katharina Fritsch.*

BELOW *Original 1907 drawings by Charles A. Platt of the pergola (left) and carriage house (right), used to guide the restoration.* OPPOSITE *Street elevation showing the restored carriage house and pergola above.*

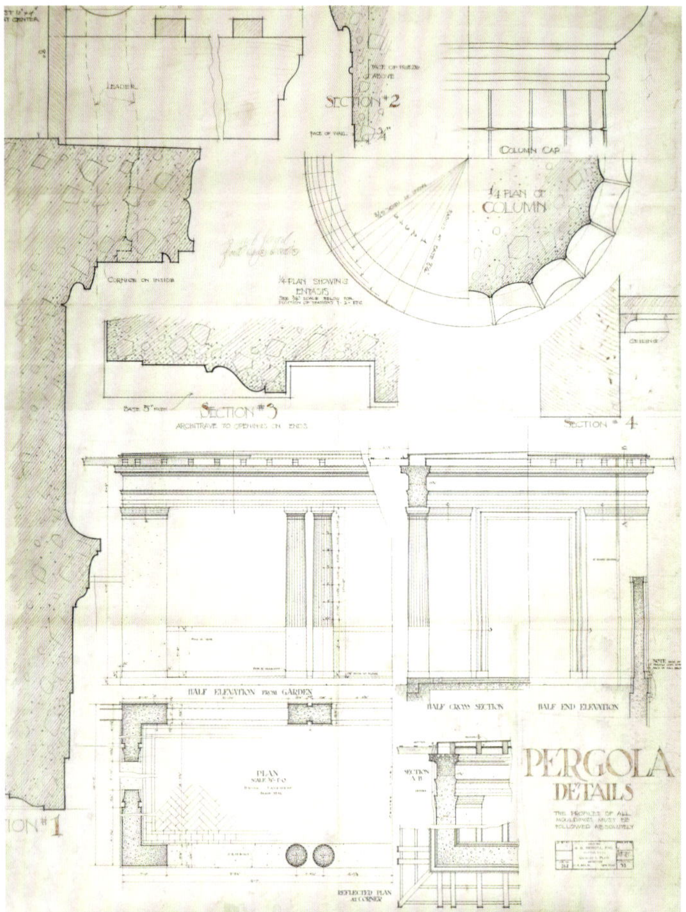

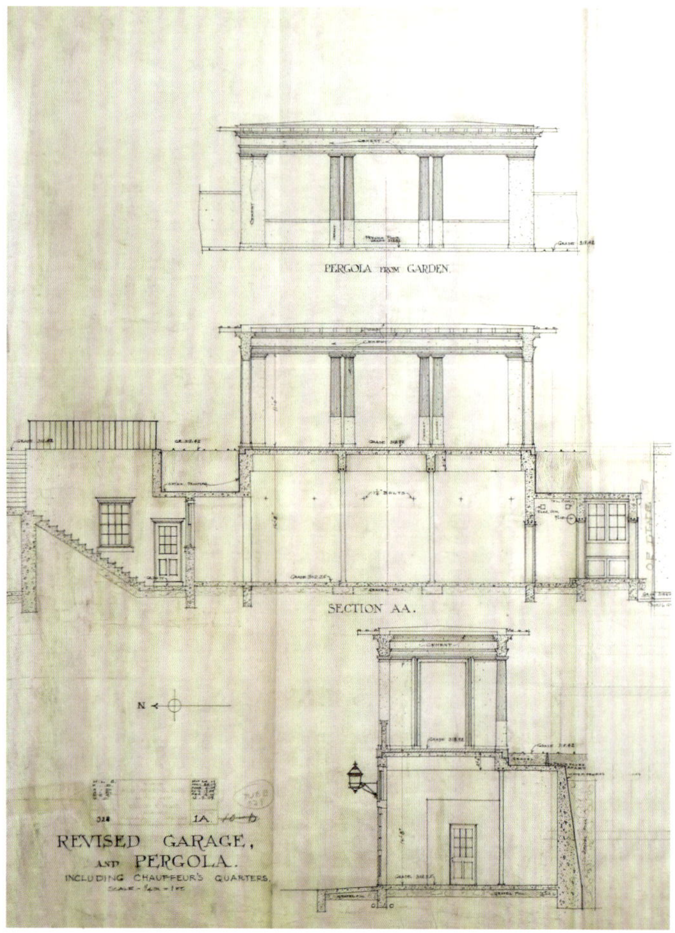

SMALL HOUSES

Since settling in the Pacific Northwest, I have designed several small houses on the islands of the Salish Sea. Most of these were conceived as weekend getaways and summer retreats. One is the painting studio of a landscape artist. Each of these houses was intended to engage sensitively with its site. Although these structures are relatively small compared to others described in this book, they embody the same principles and design processes.

In these works I attempt to balance the analysis of site energy with the intuitive evocation of the spirit of the place. In this way I hope to create an architectural language suitable to the environment of the Pacific Northwest, characterized by evergreen forests, moss-covered outcrops of bedrock, the quality of light in its northerly latitude, and the sea.

CLAM SHACK

Orcas Island, Washington — 1992

CLAM SHACK SITS CLOSE to the tideline on Orcas Island. An old clam shack on the site had burned down, leaving a foundation footprint at the edge of an old seaside orchard. Local fieldstone was used to create the massive chimney and retaining walls. The house huddles low and close to the earth, nestled into the uphill slope, so as not to exceed the height of the original shack. The interior is paneled in white-washed pine planks.

WILLOW POINT CABIN

Lopez Island, Washington — 1991

WILLOW POINT CABIN on Lopez Island sits just back from its bedrock escarpment on a rock shore. The approach follows a path through native salal, Douglas fir, and pine. The house forms a gateway to its setting. A massive chimney with both indoor and outdoor fireplaces, built of glacial field stones culled from the island, anchors the house to its position on the rocky point. Bedrock emerges in the great room and forms the hearth for the fireplace. The outdoor fireplace is a shelter edge for summer enjoyment of the long cool evenings of the Pacific Northwest. The body of the great room has two wings, each with a bedroom that takes in light from three sides. The material palette of weathered cedar and local stone mirrors that of the surrounding woods.

SHARK REEF RETREAT

Lopez Island, Washington — 2006

BELOW *The living room's bay window looks upon an ancient fir tree in the foreground and south across the Strait of Juan de Fuca.*
RIGHT *A large bay window and a roof cupola flood the interior with light.*

SHARK REEF RETREAT was designed to sit on a bedrock shelf looking out across the Strait of Juan de Fuca to the Olympic Peninsula. An ancient Douglas fir tree, windblown into a gnarled mass, holds the center of the site plan. The building wraps around the tree and attaches to an old cabin that predated the new work. The retreat's great room is conceived as an overscaled bay window looking out to sea, with the ancient tree as its focal point.

ARTIST'S STUDIO

Vashon Island, Washington — 2004

BOTTOM LEFT *The studio spans between two exisiting sheds to form a courtyard.*
BELOW *The artist Vicki Adams in her studio.*
OPPOSITE *The courtyard, paved with antique granite cobbles and millstones, provides a spatial antithesis to the work space.*

ARTIST'S STUDIO was conceived as a utilitarian space for landscape painter Victoria Adams. Although it is not a dwelling, this project, like the others in this section, is a personal creative retreat. Vashon Island, site of the studio, still has remnants of its agricultural past in the form of old farmhouses and barns. The studio was conceived as a barn form, connecting to an existing tractor shed and to a work shed to form three sides of an outdoor courtyard.

MASSACRE BAY BEACH HOUSE

Orcas Island, Washington — 2010

RIGHT *A new corner window overlooks the bay.*

ON A LARGE FAMILY RETREAT on Orcas Island with several houses, there was a small beachside cabin. This cabin was slated for demolition, but due to its nonconforming proximity to the protected shoreline, it was renovated as a guest house. Through the act of saving this remnant of the history of an old camp, the family compound is imbued with the spirit of simplicity at the place of arrival. A new corner window, overlooking the bay, transforms the old cabin by means of a change in scale. A new stone fireplace, built from native fieldstones, is the center of gravity of the cabin.

PANORAMA ROCK CABIN

Lopez Island, Washington — 2005

THIS HOUSE INCORPORATED the remnant turret of a small cabin, hand built by one of the clients. On a complex topography of bedrock outcroppings and several substantial existing fir trees, the house plan evolved into a Y form with three wings: a kitchen wing, a bedroom wing, and a studio wing. The original turret was kept as the nexus of the plan. Each wing is separated from the others by whale-like rock forms emerging from the earth. The wings assume an organic movement as they weave like tentacles among the rock outcrops. Each wing terminates in a large window, taking in the specific perspective on the landscape. The kitchen wing terminates in a large south-facing window bay looking out toward the Strait of Juan de Fuca.

ACKNOWLEDGMENTS

I HAVE HAD THE ENCOURAGEMENT and assistance of many people during my four decades of design practice. I wish to express my deep gratitude and appreciation to my senior associate Andrea Ermolli, who has worked with me for the last two decades. His talent, expertise, and joyful approach to work have contributed immensely to our creative collaboration and to the realization of the projects shown here, as well as many others. Andrea's photographic art, with his lens most often aimed at the stars in his remarkable astrophotography, is displayed on many of this book's pages.

The production of this book has been a collaboration with, among others, Gordon Goff of ORO Editions, who proposed the idea of a career retrospective; my editor Clare Jacobson, who helped me give form to these words and rough ideas; and graphic designer Pablo Mandel. My staff members Jon Junker and Michelle Murphy have worked tirelessly assembling and preparing images from the archives, while at the same time executing our current architectural projects in collaboration with other members of our great team, Peter Sweeney and Anton DeBiasi. Former studio managers Annie Gormley, Linda Beeman, Cheryl McIntosh, and Shelly Leavens all contributed to the production of this creative work.

No teacher was more important to my development as an artist than Mary Kring Risley at Wesleyan University. I began my architectural practice in the mid-1980s with the encouragement of Ptarmigan Teal, who recommended that inexperience was no reason to hold back from my dream; and of Rich Haag, my friend and mentor, who gave me a desk in his own office in which to begin. Other family members—including Penny Holden, John Teal, Libet Johnson, and Ed Sullivan—offered their confidence and their architectural projects to me as a young architect, and they did not allow the delicacy of family relationships to interfere with their enthusiasm to work together on their homes.

As a traveling fellow of the Thomas J. Watson Foundation in 1973, my year in Japan was fundamental in my developing ways of seeing and of understanding a larger world. For this seminal adventure at the age of twenty-one, I will always be profoundly grateful. I was welcomed with open arms in a foreign land and entrusted as an apprentice in its arts, traditions, and culture. To my sensei, Tatsuzo Shimaoka, and to his family, I bow

The American Academy in Rome granted me a stay as a visiting artist in 2008 in order to explore the narrative quality in ancient architecture and pottery. To the academy, I am grateful for the time and space in which to work and for the rich fellowship it provided.

I am humbly aware of the hundreds of people with whom I have collaborated over the years: clients, family members, my architectural staff, landscape architects, interior designers, builders, artisans, and artists. All have shared with me their creativity, their kindness, and their encouragement. I thank them all.

CATALOG OF SELECTED WORKS

MERRILL COURT TOWNHOUSES
Location: Seattle, WA
Date completed: 1986
Architect of record: Ibsen Nelsen, FAIA
Project architect: Stephen M. Sullivan
Photographer: Benjamin Benschneider

LOAFING SHED
Location: Millbrook, NY
Date completed: 1985

PORTAGE BAY TWIN HOUSES
Location: Seattle, WA
Date completed: 1988
Contractor: Jim Jacobson
Photographer: Jim Fanning

TUNTURI FARM
Location: Huntington Center, VT
Date completed: 1988
Staff: Mary McCrea
Interior designer: Michael Tedrick
Contractor: Dudley Rood

LIGHTNING TREE FARM RESIDENCE
Location: Millbrook, NY
Date completed: 1989
Staff: Valerie Thiel, Richard Lindstrom
Interior designer: David Easton
Landscape architect: Edwin Bye
Photographer: Daniel Millstein, Tim Lee

PORTAGE BAY BOATHOUSE
Location: Seattle, WA
Date completed: 1989
Staff: Valerie Thiel

WINDERMERE RESIDENCE
Location: Seattle, WA
Date completed: 1991
Staff: Marvin Anderson, Robin Yoshimura
Contractor: Jim Strode Construction

PORT MADISON RESIDENCE
Location: Bainbridge Island, WA
Date completed: 1991
Staff: Marvin Anderson, Robin Yoshimura
Contractor: Mueller Construction

WILLOW POINT CABIN
Location: Lopez Island, WA
Date completed: 1991
Staff: Marvin Anderson, Robin Yoshimura
Photographer: Steve Horn

MEYDENBAUER BAY
Location: Bellevue, WA
Date completed: 1992
Staff: Robin Yoshimura

CLAM SHACK
Location: Orcas Island, WA
Date completed: 1992
Interior designer: Doug Rasar
Photographer: Steve Horn

BEACH DRIVE RENOVATION
Location: Seattle, WA
Date completed: 1993
Staff: Robin Yoshimura

MAISON BELLE RESIDENCE
Location: Seattle, WA
Date completed: 1993
Staff: Robin Yoshimura
Contractor: Jim Dow

DENNY BLAINE RESIDENCE
Location: Seattle, WA
Date completed: 1993
Staff: Dan Peterson, Robin Yoshimura
Interior designer: Ken McKinnon
Landscape architect: Kemper Iversen
Contractor: Lease Crutcher Lewis
Photographer: David Story

SINCLAIR ISLAND CABIN
Location: Sinclair Island, WA
Date completed: 1993

LAURELHURST POINT RENOVATION
Location: Seattle, WA
Date completed: 1994

SUNNYSIDE FARM
Location: Woodinville, WA
Date completed: 1995
Staff: Peter Conard, Lydia Marshal,
Robin Yoshimura, Richard Lindstrom
Interior designer: Maryika Byskiniewicz
Contractor: Jim Strode Construction
Photographer: David Story

HIGHLANDS RENOVATION
Location: Seattle, WA
Date completed: 1995
Staff: Cheryl Hughes, Richard Lindstrom
Contractor: Krekow-Jennings

SPRING HILL RESIDENCE
Location: Seattle, WA
Date completed: 1995
Staff: Lydia Marshal, John DeForest
Contractor: Charter Construction
Landscape Architect: John Furtado
Photographer: David Story

SUNNYSIDE BARN
Location: Woodinville, WA
Date completed: 1995
Contractor: Jim Strode Construction
Photographer: David Story

LAKE WASHINGTON RESIDENCE
Location: Seattle, WA
Date completed: 1996
Staff: Marvin Anderson, Richard Lindstrom,
Robin Yoshimura, John DeForest
Interior designer: Michael McQuiston
Contractor: Edifice Construction
Watercolorist: W. G. Hook

LAKEVIEW TOWNHOUSES
Location: Seattle, WA
Date completed: 1990
Staff: Robin Yoshimura
Photographer: Jim Fanning

OVERLAKE DRIVE RESIDENCE
Location: Medina, WA
Date completed: 2002
Staff: Lydia Marshal, Marvin Anderson, Wayne Evars, Akiko Wade, Chester Weir, Amran Abdullah
Interior designer: Susan Young
Landscape architect: Kemper Iversen
Contractor: Charter Construction
Photographer: Benjamin Benschneider
Watercolorist: W. G. Hook

LAKESHORE DRIVE RESIDENCE
Location: Seattle, WA
Date completed: 1996
Staff: Lydia Marshall, Richard Lindstrom
Interior designer: Kristine Donavick
Landscape architect: Kemper Iversen
Contractor: Charter Construction
Photographer: Chris Eden

BROADMOOR RENOVATION
Location: Seattle, WA
Date completed: 1996
Staff: Lydia Marshall, Jennifer Bailey, Chester Weir
Interior designer: Maryika Byskiniewicz
Photographer: Fred Andrews

LAKESIDE VILLA
Location: Seattle, WA
Date completed: 1997
Staff: Marcus DiPietro, Ted Cameron
Contractor: Krekow-Jennings
Photographer: David Story

HIGHLANDS RESIDENCE
Location: Seattle, WA
Date completed: 1997
Staff: Lydia Marshall, John DeForest
Interior designer: Susan Young

PREFABRICATED ISLAND CABINS
Location: Gulf Islands, BC
Date completed: 1997
Staff: Jill Burley

PENTHOUSE RESIDENCE
Location: Seattle, WA
Date completed: 1998
Staff: Ted Cameron
Interior designer: Christian Grevstad
Photographer: Chris Eden

HUNTER BAY CABIN
Location: Lopez Island, WA
Date completed: 1998
Staff: Ted Cameron
Photographer: Steve Horn

MILLER BAY RESIDENCE
Location: Indianola, WA
Date completed: 1998
Staff: Lydia Marshall
Interior designer: Terry Hunziker
Landscape architect: Richard Pulkrabek
Photographer: David Story

ORCAS ISLAND CABIN
Location: Orcas Island, WA
Date completed: 1998
Staff: Lydia Marshall

WILLOW POINT GUESTHOUSE
Location: Lopez Island, WA
Date completed: 1998
Staff: Marvin Anderson

ASGARD RESIDENCE
Location: Medina, WA
Date completed: 1999
Staff: John DeForest, Jill Burley, Marvin Anderson, Ted Cameron
Interior designer: Terry Hunziker
Contractor: Bender Chaffey Construction
Photographers: Andrea Ermolli, David Story

NORTH CAPITOL HILL
Location: Seattle, WA
Date completed: 1999
Landscape architect: Kemper Iversen

HIGHLANDS #1 RENOVATION
Location: Seattle, WA
Date completed: 1999
Interior designer: Michael Tedrick
Photographer: David Story

LAKE WASHINGTON PENTHOUSE
Location: Seattle, WA
Date completed: 1999
Staff: Jill Burley
Interior designer: Kristine Donavick
Contractor: Joseph McKinstry Construction

LAKE SAMMAMISH RESIDENCE
Location: Sammamish, WA
Date completed: 1999
Staff: Peter Conard, Loren Supp, Jill Burley
Contractor: Jim Strode Construction
Photographer: Benjamin Benschneider

WHIDBEY ISLAND CABIN
Location: Whidbey Island, WA
Staff: Chester Weir
Date completed: 1999

BRATTLE STREET RENOVATION
Location: Cambridge, MA
Date completed: 2000
Staff: Chester Weir
Photographer: Peter Vanderwalker

FEDERAL AVENUE RENOVATION
Location: Seattle, WA
Date completed: 2001
Staff: Marvin Anderson
Interior designer: Michael Tedrick
Landscape architect: David Pfeiffer
Photographer: Benjamin Benschneider

MERCER ISLAND RESIDENCE
Location: Mercer Island, WA
Date completed: 2001
Staff: Jeff Adberg, Peter Conard, Andrea Ermolli, Chester Weir
Interior designers: Michael Tedrick, Susan Marinello
Landscape architect: Richard Haag
Contractor: Schultz-Miller
Photographers: Benjamin Benschneider, Aaron Leitz

SEARS CATALOG COTTAGE HISTORIC RENOVATION
Location: Lopez Island, WA
Date completed: 2002
Contractor: Pamela Pauly

TIDEWATER
Location: Phippsburg, ME
Date completed: 2004
Staff: Jito Da Silva
Photographer: Peter Vanderwalker

OLYMPIA BAY RESIDENCE
Location: Olympia, WA
Date completed: 2005
Staff: Jeff Adberg, Andrea Ermolli, Maria Simon
Interior designer: David Goularte
Contractor: Mark Hamilton
Photographer: Benjamin Benschneider

BROOKWOOD RENOVATION
Location: Seattle, WA
Date completed: 2003
Staff: Marvin Anderson, Andrea Ermolli, Jennifer Bailey
Contractor: Jerry Fulks

YARROW POINT RESIDENCE
Location: Bellevue, WA
Date completed: 2003
Staff: Peter Conard, Andrea Ermolli, Arlene Kissel, Loren Supp
Photographer: Benjamin Benschneider

HONEYCHURCH ANTIQUES
Location: Seattle, WA
Date completed: 2003
Staff: Andrea Ermolli
Photographer: Benjamin Benschneider

ARTIST'S STUDIO
Location: Vashon Island, WA
Date completed: 2004
Staff: Jeff Adberg, Maria Simon
Photographer: Benjamin Benschneider

WINTER BEACH RESIDENCE
Location: Medina, WA
Date completed: 2005
Staff: Jeff Adberg, Peter Conard, Andrea Ermolli
Interior designer: Susan Young
Landscape architect: Richard Haag
Photographer: Benjamin Benschneider

PROSPECT RESIDENCE
Location: Seattle, WA
Date completed: 2005
Staff: Andrea Ermolli, Cornell Chu

PANORAMA ROCK CABIN
Location: Lopez Island, WA
Date completed: 2005
Staff: Andrea Ermolli, Chester Weir
Contractor: David Chicovsky
Photographer: Benjamin Benschneider

SHARK REEF RETREAT
Location: Lopez Island, WA
Date completed: 2006
Staff: Jito Da Silva, Andrea Ermolli
Contractor: David Chicovsky
Photographer: Benjamin Benschneider

NORTHWEST LOGGIA
Location: Seattle, WA
Date completed: 2006
Staff: Andrea Ermolli, Arlene Kissel, Jito Da Silva
Interior designer: Susan Young
Landscape architect: Richard Haag
Contractor: Toth Construction
Photographer: Benjamin Benschneider

SOUTH WASHINGTON PARK RENOVATION
Location: Seattle, WA
Date completed: 2007
Staff: Jeff Adberg, Andrea Ermolli, Jito Da Silva
Interior designer: Bradley Huson
Landscape architect: Bradley Huson
Contractor: Schultz-Miller

HENRY HOUSE
Location: Medina, WA
Date completed: 2007
Staff: Marvin Anderson, Maria Simon
Contractor: Shultz Miller

MADRONA RESIDENCE
Location: Seattle, WA
Date completed: 2008
Staff: Marvin Anderson, Freya Johnson
Photographer: Benjamin Benschneider

POINT HOUSE RENOVATION
Location: Orcas Island, WA
Date completed: 2008
Contractor: Schuchart Dow

EASTSIDE RESIDENCE
Location: Mercer Island, WA
Date completed: 2009
Staff: Jeff Adberg, Peter Conard

ENGAWA RESIDENCE
Location: Seattle, WA
Date completed: 2009
Staff: Jonathan Junker, Maria Simon,
Jim Romano, Cornell Chu
Interior designer: Doug Rasar
Landscape architect: Terry Welch
Contractor: Krekow-Jennings
Photographers: Benjamin Benschneider

BRIDLE TRAILS RESIDENCE
Location: Bellevue, WA
Date completed: 2009
Staff: Peter Conard, Jeff Adberg,
Maria Simon, Cornell Chu
Contractor: Krekow Jennings
Photographer: Benjamin Benschneider

CIRCLE H RANCH
Location: Davenport, WA
Date completed: Unbuilt
Staff: Kelly Reigsecker

MASSACRE BAY BEACH HOUSE
Location: Orcas Island, WA
Date completed: 2010
Contractor: Schuchart Dow
Photographer: Benjamin Benschneider

YAKIMA RENOVATION
Location: Yakima, WA
Date completed: 2010
Staff: Peter Conard, Andrea Ermolli,
Cornell Chu
Interior designer: Doug Rasar
Contractor: Sevigny Constuction
Photographer: Aaron Leitz

HUNTS POINT RESIDENCE
Location: Hunts Point, WA
Date completed: 2011
Staff: Marvin Anderson, Andrea Ermolli, Richard Lindstrom
Interior designer: Holly McKinley
Contractor: Krekow Jennings Inc.
Photographer: Benjamin Benschneider

WASHINGTON PARK RESIDENCE
Location: Seattle, WA
Date completed: 2011
Staff: Jeff Adberg, Peter Conard, Freya Johnson, Cornell Chu
Interior designer: Doug Rasar
Landscape architect: Randy Allworth
Contractor: Lockhart-Suver LLC
Photographer: Aaron Leitz

CLIFF RESIDENCE
Location: San Juan Islands, WA
Date completed: 2012
Staff: Maria Simon, Jim Romano
Contractor: Schuchart Dow
Photographer: Andrea Ermolli

HUNTS POINT WEST RESIDENCE
Location: Hunts Point, WA
Date completed: 2012
Staff: Jeff Adberg, Andrea Ermolli
Interior designer: Karen Yttrup
Landscape architect: Richard Haag
Contractor: Toth Construction

NORTHPOINTE
Location: Hunts Point, WA
Date completed: 2012
Staff: Jeff Adberg, David Dahl, Andrea Ermolli

ORCHARD RESIDENCE
Location: Bellevue, WA
Date completed: 2012
Staff: Maria Simon, Josh Van Donge, Jim Romano

BUDD INLET RESIDENCE
Location: Olympia, WA
Date completed 2012
Staff: Jeff Adberg
Interior designer: David Goularte

CABANA
Location: Seattle, WA
Date completed: 2012
Staff: Andrea Ermolli
Interior designer: Susan Young
Contractor: Toth Construction
Photographer: Andrea Ermolli

BLUE ATLAS RESIDENCE
Location: Seattle, WA
Date completed: 2014
Staff: Andrea Ermolli, Maria Simon, Jeff Ottom, Jim Romano
Interior designer: Doug Rasar
Landscape architect: Randy Allworth
Contractor: Toth Construction
Photographer: Aaron Leitsz

Stephen Sullivan Designs

MOSQUITO PASS RESIDENCE
Date completed: Unbuilt
Location: San Juan Island, WA
Staff: Freya Johnson

GINKGO HOUSE
Location: Greenwich, CT
Date completed: Unbuilt
Staff: Maria Simon, Freya Johnson

THE LOOKOUT RESIDENCE
Location: Seattle, WA
Date completed: 2015
Staff: Andrea Ermolli, Freya Johnson, Matthew Waddington
Interior designer: Jeffry Billhuber
Landscape architects: Charles Price, Glen Whithey
Contractor: Schuchart-Dow Construction
Photographer: Aaron Leitz

ANAMCARA RESIDENCE
Location: Scottsdale, Arizona
Date completed: 2017
Staff: Andrea Ermolli, Maria Simon, Freya Johnson
Interior designer: Doug Rasar
Landscape architect: Donna Winters
Contractor: GKO Construction LLC
Photographer: Andrea Ermolli

WHISTLER MOUNTAIN RETREAT
Location: Whistler, BC
Date completed: Unbuilt
Staff: Andrea Ermolli, Peter Sweeney

HOOD CANAL RESIDENCE
Location: Seattle, WA
Date completed: 2020
Staff: Andrea Ermolli, Peter Sweeney
Interior designer: Susan Young
Contractor: Alex Abdo, Blendheim Construction
Photographer: Andrea Ermolli

SAN YSIDRO RESIDENCE
Location: Beverly Hills, CA
Date completed: 2020
Staff: Andrea Ermolli, Jonathan Junker
Interior designer: Susan Young
Contractor: Ceci Clarke Inc.

MERRILL PERGOLA AND CARRIAGE HOUSE
Location: Seattle, WA
Date completed: 2021
Staff: Andrea Ermolli, Peter Sweeney, Jonathan Junker
Contractor: DowBuilt
Sculpture: Katharina Fritsch
Photographer: Michael Stearns

WINDERMERE TERRACE RESIDENCE
Location: Seattle, WA
Date completed: Under construction
Staff: Andrea Ermolli, Peter Sweeney, Anton Debiasi, Jonathan Junker
Interior designer: LeeAnn Baker
Landscape architect: Octavia Chambliss
Contractor: Joseph McKinstry Construction

AFTERGLOW RESIDENCE
Location: San Juan Island, WA
Date completed: Under construction
Staff: Andrea Ermolli, Anton Debiasi, Jonathan Junker
Interior designer: Kylee Shintaffer
Landscape architect: Anne James
Contractor: CRB Construction

SMOKE TREE RANCH RESIDENCE HISTORIC RENOVATION
Location: Palm Springs, CA
Date completed: In process
Staff: Andrea Ermolli, Peter Sweeney

NOTES

1. Sandra Harbert Petrulionis, Laura Dassow Walls, and Joel Myerson, ed., *The Oxford Handbook of Transcendentalism* (Oxford: Oxford University Press, 2010), 177.
2. "Churchill and the Commons Chamber," UK Parliament, accessed October 15, 2020, https://www.parliament.uk/about/living-heritage/building/palace/architecture/palacestructure/churchill/.
3. Russell Page, *The Education of a Gardener* (William Collins Sons, 1962; repr., New York: New York Review of Books, 1994), 5.
4. Vincent Scully, *The Earth, the Temples, and the Gods* (1962; rvsd., New York: Frederick A. Praeger, 1969), 43.
5. Michael Meade, "Humanity at the Tipping Point," *Mosaic Voices*, accessed August 17, 2020, https://www.mosaicvoices.org/humanity-at-the-tipping-point.
6. Philip Jodidio, *Ando: Complete Works 1975–Today* (Cologne: Taschen, 2014), 708.

Sketches of an Etruscan amphora with dancing maenad, early fifth century BCE*, Museo Nazionale Etrusco, Rome, October 2008.*

Sketch of the cryptoporticus under the walls of the American Academy in Rome, October 28, 2008.

Sketch of the Villa Medici, Rome, October 25, 2008.

CREDITS

Front cover: Cliff Residence, San Juan Islands, Washington, 2012, photo by Andrea Ermolli

Back cover: Engawa Residence, Seattle, Washington, 2009, photo by Benjamin Benschneider

All drawings © Stephen M. Sullivan except the following:

59, 107, 172: W. G. Hook

All photographs © Stephen M. Sullivan except the following:

8: Emma D. Sewall, *The Fairbanks Homestead #9,* from Abbie Sewall, *Message Through Time: The Photographs of Emma D. Sewall 1836–1919* (Harpswell, ME: Harpswell Press, 1989), 8.

10, 34, 66, 98, 118: Jonathan Junker

13, 14 –26, 28, 29, 37, 69, 101, 102, 105, 108, 162–169: Benjamin Benschneider

27, 30–33, 38, 41, 42, 47–55, 84, 90, 91, 122–26, 128, 129, 131–135: Andrea Ermolli

46: Edward Curtis

56, 61, 62, 65, 87, 93–97: David Story

70, 74, 77–83, 110, 111–117, 145–149: Aaron Leitz

121: Tsuyoshi Inui

139, 143: Daniel Milstein

141: Tim Lee

151–153, 155: Michael Stearns

159, 161: Steve Horn

170: Perrin Teal-Sullivan

174–187: image credits as noted in entries